Planet Earth Today

*How the Earth and humanity developed together,
and where we're going next*

By Candace Caddick

Brightstone Publishing

First published 2010

Published by Brightstone Publishing
2 High Trees Road
Reigate, Surrey RH2 7EJ
United Kingdom

ISBN registered to me, the author, under Brightstone Publishing.

British Library Cataloguing in Publication Data
A catalogue record for this book is available from the British Library

ISBN 978-0-9565009-0-8

Printed in the United Kingdom

I would like to dedicate this book to my daughter
in appreciation for her hours of help

To Heather Caddick

Books by Candace Caddick

Planet Earth Today: How the Earth and Humanity Developed Together and Where We're Going Next (April 2010)

The Downfall of Atlantis: A History of the Tragic Events Leading to Catastrophe (May 2010)

Contents

Acknowledgements

I would like to acknowledge the help and encouragement I received from Reiki Master Jean Jones, Alison Hopkins, Justine Sharifian and other members of the UK Reiki community. I am also grateful for the help and support of my daughters and husband while I was writing this book.

Introduction

How did I come to write this book?

I am a teaching Reiki Master who studied for 10 years before being initiated in the Usui Shiki Ryoho Reiki system. During the course of the seventeen years I've been practicing my own Reiki, my ability to channel became clearer and stronger until a couple of years ago I realised I was able to see the world around me in a way that others were not. The world became populated with elementals, angels and demons; and visions of other times and dimensions. My efforts as I worked with my own archangelic guides was always to unblock and be clear, with no preconceptions of what they may say next; to stand well back and just listen. My guides introduced me to certain people they wanted me to 'fast track' where they could answer all questions immediately through channelling, so these people could be ready to play their roles now and in 2012. The people would then move on and begin their work for the Earth.

Last year the Archangels wanted to write this book about the Earth, and because of the closeness of 2012 they wanted to shine a light into the dark corners and help us to see the reality of the world we live on. The book shows a sentient planet of incredible beauty, and a human soul of light that is under attack, lied to and deceived. I felt that as long as I was learning new information when writing, information that I couldn't begin to make up, I was on track as an accurate channel. They dictated this book, which was a combination of them explaining and me questioning. We collaborated, and I would say that seven of us wrote it together. Planet Earth Today is the first of the books that the Archangelic Collective are intending to write over the coming years, and they have much more they want to teach us. The contents of the books will always be relevant to what is happening at the moment of publication.

There is one story, a golden book like a long scroll and the two books I have completed have been lifted from here and typed up. I watched the flow of golden words enter the computer until suddenly it was the last page and the book was finished. After that my daughter and I checked and checked that I had got it down right, each paragraph and line examined to see if the golden energy ran through it steadily or if it wavered indicating that it was not quite accurate. Only when we were happy was a section considered complete. Later sometimes I would add to a section more clarity, as my own understanding improved and I could put in more detail. One of the very last paragraphs written was about the poor creature in the mines of Atlantis, and I think earlier

I was not brave enough to watch his pain. I channel using a combination of sound and sight, whichever is quicker, and where it is written the best I have been writing down their words.

Sometimes it is the right time for a book to be written and read.

Section One

The Beginning of
Your Planet's Story

ARCHANGEL MELCHIZADEK

1

THE PLANET EARTH today has reached the pinnacle of its experience as the home and main player of the game of this universe. It is at a stationary point, as if resting at the top of a peak so sharp that a breath of air will send it rolling down one of the slopes. When it rolls it will roll with tremendous speed, going faster every second. At one time we thought it would never reach the peak, never reach the top and be able to stop. Although we speak of mountains and peaks in truth the Earth has been on a descent so steep and so overwhelmingly quick that we feared the stationary point would never be reached, that the earth would roll into a black hole of darkness and pull behind it everything in the known universe.

How did a game go so far, and with such speed in a direction that seemed to promise disaster for the players and the home planet for the game; and the angelic hosts playing from the point of light and love? Let the record show that the game played here was played with such thoroughness that it will not need to be repeated in this exact form. The darkness found its limits in this game; as did the light. The polarisation of light and dark could go no farther and have any value or anything new to teach the Creator about this aspect of his wholeness. The game of limitation had run to its bitter end.

The game did not stop. This precious planet, so gracefully and beautifully singing her golden song in the heavens; was captured and imprisoned. It was bound in chains, squeezed and tormented brutally by the ones who had conquered it. It circled its sun as time sped by and conditions deteriorated for it and those who lived on the planet.

There came a time when the planet was completely overwhelmed by darkness, where the forces of darkness knew that this was their home, that they were untouchable and that they could do whatever they liked here. They fed on the people and on the planet itself. They burrowed into the surface and made their home in the centre. They bred and spread outward to other planets and systems where they could increase

3

their numbers and strength. All that was beautiful and light was torn down and destroyed; or altered to serve darkness. The planet's shield, which all planets have to protect themselves, had been dismantled and destroyed. Its shield gone, there was nothing to prevent any who wished to harm it from settling on its surface and making themselves at home. It was a planet without its energetic skin, and the surface of the earth crawled as if with maggots, and the deep places contained nests of beings of darkness. And there was plenty of food for them all.

As the demons bred they feasted on war, misery, hate, and brutality, and the people changed to provide this kind of vibrational food for their capturers. They had shut down and closed faces; people with destructive habits and behaviour. It was so easy to move from this into the brutal treatment of one human to another and one sex to another and justify it with religion. Religion taught that God says this is the way to treat other humans (!); with control and power instead of love and joy. Where wars could be ignited then there would be feasting in that area, but all areas provided sustenance for the overlords.

The wars were the worst with dismembered bodies and misery; and so much heartache in the survivors left behind. Unhappy lives were spent remembering the promise of the young men who were killed. But there were more deaths in every war, more civilians killed and more agony. The agony was food for the new gods, they grew and multiplied and strengthened on the abundance of it. There never seemed to be an end to war on the planet Earth, small wars and big wars; each worse than the last.

You recognise this picture, those of you who have picked up this book. And you have blamed yourselves as a species. You believe that humanity is so weak, so apt to create darkness and turn to it. This is not a true picture of what has happened here. Mankind is a wonderful creative force, each with the power to create universes of beauty and light, joy and love. It is also blind; restricting itself to the first three dimensions. You have been such easy prey, like rabbits in a field being picked off by invisible wolves. And every time one of you had any idea that this was what was happening, and caught a glimpse of a wolf in the field he or she were captured by their fellow rabbits and locked away where they couldn't spread their visions of the truth.

Who had the power to lock them away? Where was the fear generated of all things in the upper dimensions? Fear of being seen as special or different, with slightly (and these glimpses were very slight indeed) enhanced talents. Look at your long history and see where the power lies, the power to accuse, control and punish. Lying like a blanket of darkness across the world with very few islands of light is the power of the resident church. And each church and religion spoken of here is the same, with no distinction made between Christianity and Islam, Judaism, Hinduism and all the rest of the world religions. All have removed the connection of man to their God with equal effectiveness. God is not reached by following rules but through the love in each person's own heart.

Your scientists measure light into radio waves, televisions waves, electromagnetic waves and visible light waves. We include all that and more in our definition of light; we include love as our definition of the purest form of light. Love is how you feel light in your bodies, hearts and souls. Fear is the opposite of love, not hate. Hate is an emotion, a reaction, a fear-based belief system. You carry love in your person and it shows as light, it spreads outwards and lights the way for others. The absence of light creates darkness, which is how we define fear. Humans may feel darkness in their souls through fear. It is often caused deliberately through lies, and keeps humans subdued and frozen in place with no forward movement. It is a weapon to be used against you.

A long time ago, a very long time ago, this planet was the home to a number of races who each found their connection to God through their experiences of living here on Earth in partnership with her. In the furthest distant past were five races that completed their journeys of light. Playing the game of limits and polarisation of light and dark, they became light in the end, and joined the game as players who are light and love. Within this universe of limits there were many planets hosting these games. All the games fed back to the Creator who accepted the presence of the light and the dark as aspects of wholeness. All there is, is an expression of love even if it appears to be as black as night.

As the games progressed on all the planets there was rejoicing that so much could be experienced and learned in this game. There was love, laughter and joy, grace and beauty, music and hope. There were challenges of darkness to draw out strength, courage, fire and wisdom, gentleness and compromise. Much more than this was learned and the game of restrictions in limited, linear time progressed to include subtleties unimagined before the start of the games. A balance was reached on many of these planets, and a joyfulness and wholeness radiated out from those where the game had reached a balanced and natural end. Safe beneath their shields, civilisations lived their daily lives on whole and healthy planets; as with an ever increasing vibration of light they enjoy life waiting to return to Source before the next universe begins a new game.

Some planets had a harder time than others reaching this point of balance and wholeness. There is darkness in this universe in equal measure to the light; equal in numbers, strength and power. The role of the darkness is to coax a higher reaction and a higher set of lessons from the light. It gives contrast to the light and where there is courage and bravery it is usually shown up against a canvas of darkness. The darkness fulfils its function by challenging the beings of light to pull more from their depths, to surprise themselves with their reserves of strength and compassion. Some beings of light found the dark so seductive, and so easy a river to float down that they never struggled to produce any flashes of love, light, generosity or joy. This is how the great imbalance began.

Once the imbalance began we who monitor the light in this universe found ourselves struggling to open hearts and minds to love and truth; there was too much opposition in place on some planets for these blessings to come through clearly. It was an uphill struggle with the light fighting to escape from a morass of tarry darkness. The denser the darkness became the more it was able to smother the light. There are planets where light is unrecognisable now; residents simply do not know what they are seeing and all appears dark.

Darkness can take the form of lies and misdirection, manipulation and deception. When the light of truth shows these things for what they are then there is a fair choice that can be made for the light, or for the dark. We see also the pain and suffering of war and violence as the lies and deceptions multiply and create the right conditions for these.

2

THERE WAS A time when the dark and light in this universe were in balance, a *very* long time ago, and so many eons ago that to us now it would seem like the dawn of the universe. But the universe existed for a great length of time in balance and much was learned under those conditions. The imbalance began almost imperceptibly, a little here on this planet, a little there on that one. The imbalance was not always towards the dark, sometimes it was towards the light on certain planets. Then we all stopped to watch with fascination what would happen on those planets where there was no balance, but a tipping towards light or dark. For we are watchers and learners; as are you. In our role we accept that we are mighty, perhaps the mightiest in this universe because we know our own strength and exist with our eyes wide open and a personal memory of God. We watch life on the planets and know that they are our equals, but their blindness hampers their ability to express their power. All are equals; as above, so below.

Some planets began to speed towards the light at a great rate, while others began to speed towards the darkness in a balancing way. There were planets that were full of misery and ones where there was blissful happiness. But there was always balance and we watched as the balance shifted to be shown across a wider base. Planets were balancing each other and were hosting game players who were now playing very different games. This base grew and the universe adjusted to working in this new method. Across the galaxies there was a vibrancy of life and experience as activities took place that illuminated existence in a time-limited universe. On the whole we felt that it was going well, that much was being learned that was new, that the game in progress in this universe was exciting and valuable.

There began to be a shift and a sliding, a smearing of the experience. It seemed that some planets were plummeting in freefall and that there the misery was so acute that the light planets were unable to provide the balance. One planet of light in a sector of a galaxy would be trying to balance ten, twenty, fifty or more planets that were struggling to have an experience that was wholesome. We use the word wholesome to mean a planet or person who is whole and healthy. There were many planets that were sickening, splintering and decaying. Something we had not anticipated was happening and that was the death of the planets that were hosting the populations. This was very sad as they are a noble race of beings with their own consciousness and community, with great generosity of spirit. Their playful and jubilant natures were being smothered by what was happening on their surfaces and some of them began to die; and there was nothing that we could do. When a planet dies in this universe it is dead to its kind until the final and ultimate end of the games.

Darkness was spreading through the universe and we could see that there was no longer a light and dark balance. This was opportunistic on the part of darkness, and part of their legitimate nature. We also have the right to cover a universe in light if we are able. Light and dark strive against each other to be the most prevalent. It is our role to be ourselves, to express ourselves as we are each an expression of God. But how could there be an imbalance of light and dark in this sealed universe? We began to look for the answer.

The darkness was growing the thickest around the planets that had fallen into darkness the farthest. We could see breeding of dark entities happening there where there was so much food for them, and the local populations were being devoured energetically and twisted to make the food in greater quantities and qualities for the demons that resided there. These were planets of war and terror and they were surrounded by dark angels, our counterparts, our other halves. They are as many and as varied in their types, shapes and beings as we are.

These planets of darkness had the ability to draw in the light and snuff it out, as if it had never existed. Where a connection could be made to the heart of one who lived there we would feed that heart with love and the light of joy that could be found on the other planets. But the darkness would roll over that one and the light could not reach the soul again. The dark planets contained life and species that volunteered to play a game on the surface, or sometimes inside a planet, to find out more about God by being cut off from the light completely. They learned that all is God, the light and the dark.

Some of these planets were terrible places where every quality that is not love, is not light, prevailed and filled the populations with acute misery. The dark angels, our other selves, fuelled the hatred, the pogroms and genocides, mass slaughter of other species and fouling the actual planet itself. Our efforts to break through and remind them of the light were minimally successful overall. But we never abandoned a planet or those who were living on it.

The darkness around these planets was very thick, and it laughed back at our efforts to penetrate and provide light. Once we were one, long ago before the creation of the universe, created by one who was great enough to create all of this. But we are adversaries now, and that is the rule and framework of this experience in this universe; dark versus light. We seek to cover the universe in light and the dark angels seek to cover it in dark. Do you know there are dark universes that have no light? There was no way home to the light for those many souls living there. Their game continues until all the games are done. We have also universes of light waiting for the time when they flow back to their creator and rejoin the light of All That Is.

We supported the planets of light to keep the vibration of light present in the universe. This job was becoming harder and harder for us to do successfully. After taking counsel together we began the first War in the Heavens. This was so long ago that you will have no planetary memory of this here on Earth. We invaded and fought around these planets of darkness and the light began to return as we cleared away the numbers of parasites and dark entities feeding there. We are very powerful and used our strength to remove the excess from these planets. These planets were as swimmers coming to the surface and gasping for air as they were being cleared. We then pushed the entities back through the walls of the universe to return them to the Creator. This clean-up operation lasted a long, long, time.

It was during that time that we, the angels of light began to provide a safe haven for those planets and souls that wished to withdraw from the larger game when their own game had finished in a unification of light. These planets of light chose not to continue to host multiple games and risk their own lives in support of the other beings learning about God through limitation. These are the great planets of your universe, complete in their knowledge and understanding of God. They had no need to continue to play, and no need to risk their own light in a series of games. These planets are complete and whole, wholesome and healthy with living populations of god-realised beings joined in a united soul.

9

Their presence blesses this universe with their vibration of light, holding light as a beacon in the darkness.

These safe havens allowed a balance to be regained across the universe, a wobbly, unstable balance. It never seemed to take much to push a system or planet into disease or lack of wholeness. We supported all planets and their populations as best we could. Much of value came from this period of time, lessons of precision and limits, and how much could be safely done at any one time. We never let the dark angels have so completely a free run on a planet again as had happened in the past.

This period did not last very long in the long passage of time in this universe. We could not maintain the balance everywhere although we never gave up or abandoned any planet or group of planets to darkness and always maintained a presence there. Some planets were in torment and it was heartbreaking to hear their cries for help. We do all that we are able to help such planets. We kept looking for the cause of this imbalance which should not be.

Night was falling across the vibrant life in the multi-dimensional universe, and planets were shutting down to protect themselves from the pain. In the end we found ourselves in a sleeping universe of planets and stars. As far as we could see there was life on planets that were no longer conscious. The voices and music and humming of the planets had been stilled. All connection between the spheres was broken, and all communication stopped. A community of souls had withdrawn from the existence around them.

The stars were in mourning without their comrades and elected to quietly withdraw and hibernate. They were never as deeply asleep as the planets, and they have greater strength and ability to defend themselves from attack. They began to doze off and on and we could rouse them when we needed their help and participation. Some of the stars never slept and never abandoned their planets but kept a watchful eye on their well-being. These are the mighty stars of the universe, a few of great stature and soul in every galaxy; steadfast in their holding of the light for all the other life-forms alive in their areas. Their areas of responsibility grew and grew as they kept their light intact for all to see, and to maintain and anchor that light for the benefit of all. These became known as the great central suns of each galaxy, able to support whole galaxies with their connection to light and the aspect of God that is light.

On the planets themselves there was an abundance of life; they were overflowing with life all having experiences and finding out about limits and time. The game of discovery was continued by these beings of many different types and varieties. How many different forms of life do you have on your planet alone? We devoted ourselves to guiding these life forms as best we could, always shining before them the light. Many forms chose light, truth, joy and love. As they honed their many lives and deepened their experience with the light of love they left their planets as a mass conscious soul. They were no longer individuals but had achieved union and became one. These great and completed souls are still here in this universe and we align ourselves with them and work with them as partners in the evolution of this universe. They each shine with their own particular brightness and are our dear friends. Your planet has produced five of these great souls already as life forms have incarnated and learned all they could about God through their own experiences. They have chosen different paths since leaving, but one at least is still here because of its attachment to the planet it loves. When the human race is ready to ascend it will also become one mass soul, and be free from the pain of separation from each other, blissfully reunited.

Reunited? As your animals and others on this planet are each one soul, so too is man. Mankind sought to extend its experience through separation and chose a splintering of the soul. We need not tell you that this is very far from being whole; very, very far from being whole and wholesome. Having made the choice in your distant past this planet began to host a game that was as extreme as any played on any planet in this universe. The game began to go downhill rapidly almost from the very beginning.

3

H UMANS HAVE A long and varied history on this planet Earth. You were created here from a wish and a desire on the part of your single soul to come to this exact planet and play a game of limitations. You limited yourself by splintering into shards of humanity, and when you awoke on Earth you were all strangers to one another. This was unheard of for a planetary game. Until this time all games had been played as follows: a unified soul was accepted by the planet for a game and a contract was drawn up between the two parties. This contract was based on universal law, the law that provides the parameters of all games in this universe. The soul would begin a series of incarnations and learning experiences with a deep connection between the individuals who were incarnating from one soul group. The individual lives would be lived, but their minds would share information as needed. When a life ended the body would die and the soul would rejoin the mass consciousness of the group and wait for the next incarnation. The next incarnation would begin and as the new life learned and lived there was guidance from the soul group. The soul group playing a game in this manner learns very quickly. Sometimes your scientists here have asked 'How does a flock of birds or a school of fish know how to work so closely together and move at times as one being?' At those times the flock or school has discarded their individuality and become the mass mind of their kind. They fly and swim as one.

We could immediately see that your lack of connection to each other had also cut your connection to all forms of life on this planet and to the planet itself. We could hear a great howl of loneliness from the human hearts on this planet, a howl that has never subsided. The numbers of humans incarnate could always be increased by splintering into ever smaller shards, and this had the effect of making the surface of the Earth almost boil with the mass of humanity trying to live on its surface. All separate, all alone and with a heart filled with longing to be whole.

The Earth herself was unhappy about this development. She was carrying on her surface as part of herself a vast population of beings of misery, joylessness, and hatred with all the vibrational darkness that entails. There were beings of light swimming in her oceans, and flying in her skies but their numbers began to rapidly decrease as the humans spread and killed them. She began her rapid descent into darkness herself, and over time she struggled to maintain her own connection to the light. We did not abandon her, but kept open for her a conduit to the light and love of her creator.

Back in the beginning of this experiment of splintering, humanity took a further step and divided themselves into male and female. This was at the time of Atlantis, the origin of the Garden of Eden story. The realm of Atlantis brought forth male and female and their way of reproducing the species. The beginning of this game was promising; a pleasant and fruitful land filled with souls discovering that even as splinters they could learn about themselves as an expression of God. We came and instructed them; we helped them form rules based on Universal Law to guide them in their lives. Working as men and women beneath a thick veil they still formed a cohesive whole as a society. We all watched with great interest this extreme game.

4

THIS WAS THE most astonishingly extreme game that anyone had ever conceived. Let us set down the new and unusual aspects of this game.

1. There was no connection to each other, any other form of life on the planet or to the planet itself, or to the local star.
2. The higher dimensions were hidden by a thick veil.
3. The ability to see all the angels of light and dark, the elementals (dryads, gnomes, fairies, etc.) and beings of the other dimensions was removed.
4. The players had no previous memory of all that had been learned across the long eons of this universe and were starting this game as blank and clean as an empty sheet of paper.
5. The players were prepared to play and play and play with hearts breaking with loneliness. (This was the most extraordinary of the aspects to those of us who watched.)
6. God was wiped as a memory for them; they wanted to see if they could find him from a position of complete unknowing.

I am Melchizadek, the archangel of connection to God. My function and energy provides the link to God, to pass across my bridge is to walk towards God with his light shining in your face. At the time of Atlantis I resided there in spirit, and opened healing temples through my priesthood for those humans who began to show illness in their lives due to their separation from each other. The separation was made worse by not understanding they were one and the same. These fragments of the human soul, each with the potential to be whole, were missing many aspects of the combined soul. They were aware of their own shortcomings subconsciously.

The initial healings were all for problems of the mind, there was no physical illness to speak of in the beginning. My temples were separate areas where the connection to the outer universe was accessible to those inside. When humans entered the temple space they were reunited to the vast life and connectedness of the outside universe and to the planet below. This allowed them some relief to their heartache.

While in the temple they would receive healing from my priests by lying on a table of stone that was chosen for its properties and qualities. These stone tables were filled with the energy of love and connection by me, and to rest on one was to be cradled in my arms. My priests would then perform the healing using the vibrational remedy given by God to the universe for its unbroken connection to him. I have brought back this energy in these days for its use by the population now. Mikao Usui reintroduced it to this planet over one hundred years ago and called it Reiki. Using the Reiki of Usui will let a stream of the supportive energy of the source of life itself to enter into the user and reconnect them to the universe. This is the purpose of Reiki, to connect to God. There are many on your planet now who have been initiated into 'Reiki', but I look at them and do not see Reiki energy. This is an energy that will need yet another introduction in another name. There are so few now left from the Usui introduction that carry the true energy and hold it in their souls. I urge any who wish to be trained in Reiki to go back as close as they can in lineage to that of Usui, where there are fewer steps between Usui and the Reiki Master. I would not be able to work with this channel as closely as I do if she had not trained in Reiki from one close to Usui in lineage where the Reiki came through to her intact. In this book I would like to acknowledge that there are other methods of healing that are beneficial, but I will only be talking about Reiki as that is what we introduced for the benefit of Atlanteans.

I filled my temples with priests and acolytes who were all able to heal and had been trained to a higher level in Reiki. The population all accepted their first attunements at a young age in school in the presence of their classmates and families. They would be young children of three and four. It was a big day in the life of the young child, and they were expected to practice their Reiki daily to maintain their mental and physical health. For the most part this is what happened for a very long time. The daily practice of Reiki by the Atlanteans was universal for the first three ages of Atlantis. The practice only fell away in the last age of that great civilisation.

My temples held the Reiki students with additional initiations as they proceeded on their path to become healers. The priests at that time did the initiations in the temples and schools, and taught classes in healing. I initiated my priests at that time energetically so that they were able to do my work. When I initiated my priests I selected only those who had the integrity and strength of spirit to carry an energy funnelled directly through myself from God. I am a conduit, a bridge and a connection. I am the only connection between this sealed universe and the timeless space outside. When travelling from this universe to the centre of all things, all must pass through me. It is how I connect all that is here to the Creator of this game. Another word for what I do is the Christ. When it is said 'the only way to God is through the Christ', there must be a crossing of my bridge. There are some in the history of this planet that have done so.

For a long time my temples were oases of peace for the population, and all were welcome to come and connect by resting inside the temple space in a garden, or have healing from the priests to lessen their distress. The priest would allow the energy of God, the universal life force energy, to fill the person on the table and for that time they would join God's energy, and rejoin the larger community of the universe in which they were resident. This experience of communion was enough to rebalance those who visited the temples.

One day, imagine my surprise when there was a man on the table who was physically diseased! The healers worked with this man to return him to health and were successful in their treatments. He had to come regularly and new ways of treating were devised to heal him. In the end he was returned to health. This was the beginning of the onset of physical disease, which we attributed directly to heartache and loneliness, the underlying conditions of the game.

The work in Atlantis continued to be temple-based for those of us who are Archangels of the Light. The Atlanteans were the first to call us by our present names that you know us by: Melchizadek, Azreal, Michael, Raphael, Gabriel, Uriel, and others. We were part of the daily life of the population at that time who recognised our presence by our qualities of light. And these lost and lonely souls had a connection that you today do not: each was connected to the divine source of love and light through their daily practice of Reiki. A steady golden flow touched the heart of each one so that disconnected from each other as they were; they had a connection to God. This was the flow of energy into their life that made their lives healthy from birth to death and allowed a simple contentment within the parameters of the game. While this time lasted we had no real fears that this game could go so far wrong, or cause a leakage of damage that would begin to trail across the universe.

5

TIME PASSED AND the Atlantean society, which had been a rural, pastoral society to begin with, altered. Our temples were rebuilt in the elaborate and sumptuous forms that you associate with ancient temples today. The choice of stone was marble, cold and hard where before we had used whatever materials were local, and wood by choice. By using wood we were making use of the love present in trees, who are great fountains of love frozen in the form of wood. When a tree was ready to end its life in old age we would wait and pick it up off the forest floor and honour it for the love it had expressed during its life. The trees allow a home to be built in safety on this planet; they form the strength of the walls and the sky is the roof. The walls therefore are made of love. In all the long years of this planet, through all the races that have lived here the trees have held love in their forms and radiated it out to all. All lesser plant life is able to live and express themselves in their many ways because the trees hold them in strong arms of love. They are a gift of God to those who live here. Are they found on other planets? On some they are found in all their glory and honoured for what they embody.

We did not care for the new temples as it seemed that the motivation for rebuilding had nothing to do with the function of the temples. The temples had been simple with pleasant gardens and covered spaces to keep out of the rain and wind. The new temples were showy and prestigious and we wondered why they felt this was needed for us. There was a darkness lying in pockets now on the face of Atlantis, and twisting tendrils of it were winding around our new temples. The darkness could never enter our space there, where we kept the connection open to the universe and all that is. But the darkness seemed to be climbing up the walls as time went by.

Outside the temples there was darkness growing in many places and locations, and for the first time we could see darkness in some hearts where the golden thread of connection no longer existed. There was nothing we could do to force a reconnection for those who chose not to have one. These people were beginning to behave very differently to the ones whose hearts were filled with love. They behaved as if their actions only mattered to themselves and could not affect another human, or hurt another human. It was as if the human was so alone that they were the only living human being walking on the face of the planet. As if they did not need to consider anything other than their own wishes and desires. But they had noticed the others living with them, and what they desired in many cases was for everyone else to fall in with their wishes and plans, and not get in the way. They looked for ways to make that happen.

What are we talking about here? We are talking about the power to control people and have them do as you wish, so that you can do exactly what you want at all times. Those who sought to live like this thought this sounded like a desirable way to live; after all they had no connection of any kind to the others around them. Not a real connection, heart to heart, and heart to God. How do you make people allow you to do whatever you want? Hurt them, and make them fear you and what you will do to them.

It began with a few in some locations behaving like this, forcing others to obey them through fear. These locations, without exception, were the city areas where the connection to the planet was the weakest. The planet at that time was the happy hostess to the game, and was purring along with her pleasure in helping another soul learn more about their connection to God. This happiness was apparent in the green hills and fertile valleys and there was an energy exchange that regularly took place between the Earth and the people. She supported their feet as they walked and gave them a place to live for the duration of the game. She was content with her role. This contentment was absorbed by those who spent their lives and time in the rural areas and on the seas as sailors. The sea had such a liquid, laughing quality that a high proportion of the population were sailors for a living or for recreation. This vibration was brought ashore by those who spent their time at sea.

Under the continent of Atlantis lived the crystal kingdom of sentient crystals, living their lives as crystals do, in a continuous exchange with the planet. The role of this kingdom was to clarify earth energy as it passed through each crystal in a two-way flow. The energy that the crystals passed to the planet was made up of the energy showered onto the outer planetary surface from the stars in the universe, combined with the energy of the species that lived on the surface. The flow back through the crystals was of the love and nurturing energy of the planet. This energy was grounded into the crystals and released back to the life above. Here was a partnership of life, crystal life and planet that allowed all to grow and share the experiences of each other.

6

T HE CRYSTALS OF Atlantis have had much written about them by other authors. We want to fully tell the story of the crystal and mineral kingdom of Atlantis now in this book, as it is relevant to the world as it is now.

In the beginning of the continent of Atlantis a complementary relationship existed between the crystal life and the planet Earth. There was respect, love and a close partnership; and energy that flowed like a current through the daily lives of the crystal life forms. These crystal lives seemed to some to be static and unfeeling, after all humans cannot observe the vitality and life that is present in the crystals. But these great crystals were seeded by the stars and angels themselves, placed on Earth as representatives of the forces of light. They are able to hold incredible depths of love and intelligence; and they communicate with each other as a whole being, a complete consciousness present in Earth's physical reality. They had completed their own game. All crystals on the planet are as much one being as your fingers are part of you. Unlike your fingers the crystals were also able to maintain their autonomy and act as individuals. This allowed them to gain greater experience as a life-form and soul than they would have as a single unit with no ability to separate.

As individuals they would converse and take council together; and they would agree policy and actions. Information was brought from the individual crystals into the whole consciousness of the crystal family of beings. In earlier days there had been a time when the crystals were the dominant life form on the planet. This gives you an indication of how alive they are in their own way. Always they worked in partnership with the other life forms on the planet, for the good of the planet. This allowed the other life forms an accelerated learning experience, they learned more, faster and ultimately finished at a higher level. When each soul group moved into their ascended state the crystals remained behind by choice. This allowed them to meet planetary needs and the needs of those living on the planet.

At the time the humans entered to begin their game the crystals were the wise, old residents of this planet. They had participated in every game just by being present, and they had learned much by observing life. Some small crystals had had exciting experiences as friends and companions to the other races as they evolved, living in their homes and being carried around often as jewellery. These crystals were able to input much into the collective crystal consciousness. The crystals hummed with life and energy, enjoying all their experiences. Any of you who have lived with crystals in your home will know something of this already. These tiny offshoots of the planetary crystals are members of the greatest soul group here at this time and there is much they can teach you. Allow your crystals to sleep by your bed at night and this will enable you to learn from them. When you are asleep you are more receptive to what they have to share with you. If we could see crystals by the bedsides of all humans we would consider that a blessing. All crystals would like to perform this function.

This planet set a new blueprint that many wish to copy the next time a new universe is formed. You see the brilliant colours of a blue and green Earth from space in your photographs. We see that and more: a glittering planet travelling through the universe. What we see when we look at this planet is love and brilliant shininess. It sparkles with light and love as its crystals and crystalline energy reflect the light of the stars. The largest crystals are, to this day, so deep in the earth that they have never surfaced or met any of the other life forms living on the planet. They are connected, and their energy flows through the spaces between their physical forms. You live on a world that is filled with crystalline energy; crystalline energy flows through you all your days. We consider this one of the qualities of the planet Earth that makes it so endearing. The planet itself allowed its physical form to host this race of beings; no other planet did in any part of the universe. . This is what makes the planet special in our eyes; its willingness to accept in love the crystals from the beginning, and their relationship during all this time that has passed.

Allowing the crystals to be placed into its structure changed the nature of the planet from the beginning. It was an act of love and generosity, willingness to share and a confidence in the outcome of all its games. The fibre and core of this planet had been seeded with light from the start. This planet had no wish to slide into the darkness and took steps to be made of light itself. Because of this it was willing to host some difficult games that other planets declined, and came through each of them with its brightness undimmed and a soul group that had explored its game of limitation to the end. This caused others of the planetary family to turn their attention to planet Earth, to see how generosity and love had affected all the games here from the beginning. The planets' own initial choices at the beginning of its time was the key to its ability to lift these other soul groups higher than they could have anticipated at the beginning of their games. This was astonishing, and the successful outcomes here were beyond all predictions. All who observed took note of the success of this way of working. When the human soul group came with such a daring and radical game proposal all in the planetary family thought this was the one planet who could host it successfully.

Planet Earth is unique in this universe due to its hybrid nature absorbing the crystal life forms as part of its own body. We are looking at a planet with two consciousnesses entwined, each greater than they would be if they were on their own. There is an exquisite intelligence to this planet, sharpened by everything it learns by hosting the crystals. In addition to this is the loving heart of the planet. We can see this planet's own trajectory towards the light as it learns by hosting the various games. When the grand game in this universe is wound up, planets that have hosted and learned all they could learn will be the ones to teach the others about love, joy, life and God. These precious and loving life forms, which seem so large to you that you think they are not alive but just balls of gas and dirt, are the ones who are allowing all the learning to take place by hosting the games. As the eons of this universe speed by limited by time and space, the planets themselves learn. They are playing the game at their own level and learning about their Creator through their experiences. All of these lessons will be funnelled back to the Source at the end, allowing God to know more about life, and how life is lived when limited by time and space.

This game on Earth, your game, began a dark epoch in the Earth's history which we will have to fully explain in later chapters. The game that began in Atlantis led into a descent into darkness for this bright planet.

7

THE CRYSTALS DREW energy from the earth and lived on pure universal life force energy; they contained this energy in solid form. Because the life energy was concentrated in the crystal kingdom the crystals themselves were a source of power and energy for the new humans, instead of fossil fuels. They had played this role before for the other soul groups that had finished their games and moved on into light. The quality of their energy and light was of the highest quality, the frequency of their vibration was strong enough to radiate out and be a source of fuel for the farthest flung dwellings. This energy caused no diseases as the modern forms of vibration can, but was a source of completeness and wholeness for the land and people who lived on it. Crystalline energy was of the Earth, and the Earth's energy was from the universe. Universal life force energy comes from the Creator of this universe. It is the energy that provides life and connection back to the Source. Every planet and star is connected and nourished by this energy, every life form lives because of it. It showers down onto each and every planet at all times. You think here that you have life because of the sun's light reaching the Earth every day. The sun itself lives because of the energy of the Source of all. There is more to life than scientific explanations. Life has life energy, all life is connected to this energy, and it connects all living life forms in the universe in an unbreakable bond.

You are approaching a time when the crystal energy will be renewed. There are those who know how to restart it that are waiting for the right time to begin the process of restarting the Earth's generator. What needs to be done is being done; the steps are being taken to awaken and clean the crystals of millennia of darkness that dims their light. When all the preparations have been completed the crystals will once again be able to supply power from the Earth itself for the comfort of humans. When that day comes the way of seeing your lives will have changed so that you are ready and able to accept this energy and partnership with the Earth once more. That day will not come upon you suddenly, but will be part of a renewal of your commitment to the health and well-being of this planet you live on. Until that fundamental change has filtered through your lives and ways of living here the crystals will not be providing you with energy.

Atlantis was not one island somewhere in the middle of an ocean, but an island within an archipelago. In the heart of the main island of Atlantis were the generator crystals shining with a bright white light of love and clarity. Working together with the earth the crystals would focus the abundance of the earth's energy through themselves, and the energy would pour out of them. The quantity of energy provided by the crystals would be quite staggering by today's standards of meagre output. There was enough energy to provide for all conceivable needs, and there was much that flowed out unused to be recycled. Once on the surface and present in the generator crystals the energy was drawn away through a series of smaller crystals across the land into the homes and places where energy was needed on all of the islands. The crystals were willing to do this as it was within their capabilities. In their love they desired to provide the energy so that other life forms could have the use of it. The energy was used to warm their homes and keep them well and comfortable. There were other uses before Atlantis, but none of them had ever given cause for alarm in the past. This was about to change.

8

THE COMMON EXPERIENCE of a soul group is the comfort and connection of the individual incarnate members of the group. They don't know what it is to be lonely for another of their species as they are fully connected to them at all times. They advance together with each individual adding their experiences of what they are busy learning into the group consciousness. This allows them a full participation with the lives of all their kind, and the connection of the others comes back towards them as they live day to day. The flow goes both ways for the good of the soul group.

On other planets all life elected to incarnate as whole souls with a number of members on the planet at the same time. There would be a rising up of the soul together, or a sinking of the soul together. This applies to the human soul also. On these planets sometimes a game of experiences would be played very quickly as a group rose and returned to their one whole soul, or dropped and dropped until the game ground to a halt in darkness. Sometimes when a game ends in darkness for the planet and species on it there is little that happens to improve the situation, and nowhere else the game can go. As there is a limit to light and rejoining into one, there is a limit to dark and staying separate. This is, after all, a universe of limits.

Now when this happens on a planet that it ends up in darkness and stasis, we surround that planet with a barrier of light so it will not spread over the rest of the planets. This has been going on for the duration of the game in this universe, that we quarantine planets. It is something we do with our free will and is part of our angelic game. We play the same game of limits and free will as does the rest of the universe, but we play above and you play below. Is one better than the other? The games run side by side and we chose not to play blindly but with our eyes open and obeying the universal laws. And we are light ourselves and do not chose to play as dark; but see it as something to be reversed and transformed wherever we find it. This has led to combat between those of us who are angels of light, and our counterparts who are angels of dark inside this universe.

These days there are a large number of planets who have reached a point of equilibrium with the forces of dark and light in their populations. Life on these planets has an edge of striving; striving for the light and/or striving for the dark. The balance sways a little between the two but there is an enhanced experience to living on these planets. The dark draws forth from the light the greatest effort to grow ever brighter. The dark increases as the light increases. So we are talking about wars and murders, acts of bravery, creations of beauty and goodness and self-sacrifice. We monitor these planets with very great care as these are the planets where the light shines the brightest and which comes the closest to our own fire and light. Always we watch for a falling away, a sign that the planet is struggling to maintain balance.

9

WHEN THE EARTH was formed by a swirling gas cloud it was seeded with crystals as described earlier. There was a dance between the crystals and the Earth while the planet was first forming. The vibrations of the dance are still part of her energy; the joy of that dance is still forming your world. Remember this when you think of her.

When the earth agreed to host the human game of blindness and separation the crystals were observers of the agreement. They had no prearranged role or function but are trusted to know what to do for the best in service of the light. They chose to emerge on the continent of Atlantis in a powerful form; literally providing power for the humans. In their wisdom and love they chose to generate power by circulating through themselves the abundant energy of the planet; running it in a closed loop of energy where none was squandered. There are ways to do this if you are working in harmony with crystals, allowing them to set up the system and cooperating with their instructions. These power loops had a return system back to the planet itself for the completion of the cycle. When energy was used by the people it was captured in an ethereal grid system and not allowed to escape the planet into space. This is far different from what is happening here today, where the planet is haemorrhaging energy into space; drained of its very life. It is crucial that this is understood, that the planet has a life and a life's blood, and this is being stolen from her and reducing her ability to live.

The closed loop energy system allowed the necessary power for the humans to live with light and warmth, and quickly allowed them to 'progress'. We watched what they called progress with alarm as it did not involve love, respect for other humans, animals, planet or anything else you can think of. These were the most stunted and useless beings we had ever come across in the universe. They began their game with the plan of finding God through blindness and separation; they took over a planet and had no forward movement. They swarmed in an aimless manner like ants on a summer's day before the new queens fly away to establish new nests. The swarming had no such natural end, but just continued with no purpose until the end of that continent.

We decided that we, the archangelic beings of this universe, would establish our temples and healing centres and begin instructing these new and innocent beings. These beings had the potential to cause grievous harm not only to this planet but to the wider universe. The universal balance is delicate and in this type and quality of planet we were close to the point of balance between light and dark. It is not about areas of space, but about qualities and characteristics of energy. This was a planet with an established success rate of bringing soul groups to light. She is more than what she does; however, she is an enlightened being herself. This sweet-natured soul welcomed all other souls to her and committed herself to their games and experiments that would help the Creator learn more about himself. We could see that of the two parties to the contract, the planet and the people, that the planet was the one in jeopardy, as once the game began she would have to let it run its' course. There is little a planet can do once a game has begun and the terms agreed. The planet was in the contract as the player with no back-up or help if things began to go wrong.

Our role in this universe includes caring for the living life forms that are the planets. When everything is over and all is returned to the Source, the planets will be celebrated as the ones who made the greatest contributions and the greatest sacrifices. If we could give instruction and begin a movement towards the light to the new populations, the game could continue with hope for another soul group realising their goals, giving some point to what the planet was generously hosting. When we established the temples in the new continent of Atlantis we were selecting the area where the humans were concentrated, although this was not their only area of settlement.

The temples were situated in many places to serve the local peoples in their villages and towns, not too dissimilar to your network of churches. Our temples were open at all times and there was much coming and going to reconnect energetically to the wholeness and love present in the greater universe. This is where the planet breathed, through these temples; here and where there were no humans dwelling. Everywhere the humans were living there were the beginnings of pockets of stifling darkness lying across the surface of the Earth. We saw this with sadness as we had seen this before on other planets and knew that the Earth was in for a difficult time. The blanketing with darkness of a planet cuts it off from help, and help for those living on its surface. What is the origin of this blanket of darkness? This darkness originates with our brethren, the dark angels, who are present throughout this universe just as we are.

At this time these pockets were not widespread as the Atlanteans were concentrated on their own land. As the continent began to become more thickly settled with humans and their herd animals the temples and some of the wilder mountain ranges maintained the open, two way connection with the universe. The peaks of the mountains at that time had not yet been turned to darkness as they are today.

What does it mean to have access to the universe, and why is this important? The universe holds flow, and this is the opposite of stagnation. There is movement and progress in the universe made up of many small changes on a vast number of life systems. These life systems are able to be connected with one another through the movement of life itself as it swirls through the planets and spaces between. When a planet is being starved of life by the population living on its surface we look for ways to maintain some conduits to the planet of life force, so it reduces the chance of the death of the planet. Sometimes this is through the population itself, and sometimes through the structure of the planet using what is there already that resonates the most with the universal life energy. In the case of this planet we used the mountains and the inherent qualities of stone contained therein. Because the stone in the mountains is part of the mineral kingdom we work closely with it on this planet. At the time of Atlantis we had only the mountains and the mineral kingdom, and the temples of the archangels.

We felt that this was not going to be enough in the long run to keep the planet nourished with the flow of the universal life force and we were very concerned about its' life. There were far too few places of connection so we set about devising alternate methods of funnelling universal life force energy into Earth. The method we chose to experiment with was to use the dominant life force at that time; the rapidly spreading human population. We instructed them in how to draw in the life energy into their bodies in the form you call Reiki as a sacred task. As they were filled with this energy daily they were able to help us hold it on the earth as a golden blanket. When they were adepts at this, by the time they had reached the age of eleven, they were taught to release it downwards into the planet itself. For a long time this not only worked well, but it began to reverse some of the darkness growing on the Earth.

The regular practice of Reiki was something the entire Atlantean population did daily. They understood that it was their connection to life, and the planets' connection to life and the universe. This connection was known to be what maintained their health and the health of their crops and animals. Let us be clear about this, by daily practice of Reiki these disconnected, blind humans had connected to the Source of Life as individuals. Although a distant connection, it was where their soul group was able to meet and share their experiences in a limited way. The collective consciousness enjoyed by other soul groups had not been chosen for this game, but this small trickle of meeting in the distant Source was helpful, nourishing to the soul and felt through the lives on Earth.

They did not worship the Earth or Earth mother in those days, but they honoured her for her presence and willingly grouped together to channel Reiki into her, to help supply her with life. These groups met regularly and often, and could be large, covering great areas. People would come and take a seat on the ground in a circle and invite the Reiki to flow through them into the ground as a group. The effect of this was to open a portal to allow the energy through as large as the circle that was seated. While this was taking place the people were being filled with Reiki for their own benefit also, but there was always enough Reiki for that. The amount coming roaring through these healing circles was astonishing. It was drawn through in a torrent like a river and the Earth was allowed to receive it and use it as she needed. These happened frequently, and with regularity in many parts of Atlantis daily. All above the age of eleven would participate and the people who lived on the planet interacted with her so that she would remain nourished and healthy, and provide a healthy home for them. At this time we looked with satisfaction upon the arrangement.

These circles were also seasonal and cyclical to fit in with the rhythms of the year. The largest circles were joyous times, filled with laughter, drumming, dancing, food and celebration. They were never quiet even when small, but the outside of the circle would be held by those who wished to hold the Reiki energy for a while, and the inner circle would be filled with musicians, dancers and others moving between their friends laughing and talking. All loved the joy and purpose of these circles so dearly that they were anticipated with great joy by the communities, they were never a duty or a chore, but always a pleasure. We see the contrast with your religious observances today, particularly the lack of joy that is involved in your worship, as if it did not belong there. Joy and love, these express the same qualities of God. It is difficult to love without joy, and difficult to have joy without love. Remember this and seek out joy in all its hiding places and bring it into the light. Share it, dance with it, and throw it into the air to travel on the breezes.

Picture the people walking together from their houses, families with bowls of food to share, the musicians carrying their instruments. Everywhere was the sound of happy people talking. Often this would be at twilight and they would go to the open area where they usually met to sit in a Reiki circle. Someone would light a bonfire that had been prepared and some food would be put in to cook in the centre of the circle. Others who were ready would begin the circle by drawing though the Reiki while sitting and talking with their friends and companions. When the music started they would move out to dance in the centre in friendly groups while others would replace them on the edge. There would be coming and going to the food so that all would eat. As the hours passed they would continue the party, because that is what is was, and all the time the people would be bringing through Reiki and grounding it into the Earth. This is what the local circles were like. During the year the chance was there for some very large gatherings for special occasions, such as harvest time. When these times came around it was a pleasure to join in larger groups and have all day celebrations with neighbouring villages. Always the Reiki came through to energise the people and the Earth. The larger the circle the more Reiki could be brought through, and as long as there was a circular shape around the edge it would be effective. Sometimes the gaps could be quite large, but it would still work as a focus and a portal for the Earth to receive the universal energy she required.

The energy was brought through in this way for the first three ages of Atlantis, which was a very long time. We watched and saw that these practices; the daily treatment and the communal circles were enough to maintain life and health for the planet. The people were whole and connected to the Source of life in this universe. There was still darkness pushing, always pushing to tip the balance and smother the Earth in dense dark slime, but this was not being allowed to happen. Instead there was equilibrium, and as we have said, a planet with both the light and the dark is where the light shines the brightest. This is how things stood as the Fourth Atlantean Age began.

The communal practice of Reiki was a central bond for the members of the communities. They shared in common their dedication to wholeness and assisting the planet who gave them a place to live and provided them with energy. The relationship between all these life forms was based on love and respect for one another, and care and concern for the well-being of all who lived here. The people were learning about themselves, about their connection to All That Is, and their responsibilities as incarnate souls. We began to hope that there would be a worthwhile outcome from this extreme game. We were still concerned for the safety of the Earth and the other life forms living here, the animals and all those of the higher dimensional realms known as elementals. During the ages that Reiki was the daily practice there was a healthy development of progress for the human race. This was the golden age of Atlantis, the Garden of Eden before the fall.

The days of Atlantis were long and peaceful, and the shadow and the trouble that came to that continent were sudden and swift. It is necessary to learn about the fourth and last age of Atlantis to fully understand the origin of the problems that beset this planet now.

10

AS I CONCLUDE my opening section the important points I want to get across are these: (1) Humans are wearing blindfolds and can see only the tiniest part of what is happening around them and are easily deceived. (2) The idea that everything is provided here for humans to use or abuse because it is their "right" is harmful and incorrect. (3) All is not lost, yet. (4) We pin our hopes on many of you remembering your past and wishing to reconnect to the Earth in partnership. (5) All this is in your own hands, we can only advise you.

The days of Atlantis were long and filled with many lifetimes of your kind. There were many lives of the type you enjoy now where people were busy and worked and had families. When the end came it came with shocking speed, a deluge as the land sank and most lives, young and old, were lost. We were the ones who created that deluge for the good of this planet. We would be sorry to do anything like this again, but we have the power to do so. Until we know that this planet is once again safe we are watching carefully how you as a soul keep your side of the contract. The Archangel of Light will continue with the story of the Fourth Age of Atlantis.

Section Two

The War Between the Angels of Light and Dark

ARCHANGEL OF LIGHT

1

THE LIGHT BEGAN to fade in earnest in the Fourth Atlantean Age. What had begun as shadow in hollows escaped and spread and the land was covered in darkness. The people forgot that there had been another way of living based on mutual respect and joy; they believed if they didn't look out for themselves no one else would. This was a profound change from the way the humans had interacted with each other, all the other life forms present on the planet, and the planet itself.

You must understand that there is a striving between the angels of light and the angels of dark. We are each attempting to cover the universe in our own vibration; to end with the universe either completely light, or completely dark. This is our hourly struggle that is played out across the stars and galaxies. We have those who are our allies, those who were born bright and shining; and they have those who are their allies, putrid and rotting, bringing black slime to cover the light. This is their nature and who they are, and they are our equals.

The universe began as an opening in the space surrounding the Creator, a blossoming from an initial thought into an ever-growing shape. You have to imagine a number of pinpricks in the dark vastness of the void, and a number of universes. We were the architects and designers of the new universes, designed to help the learning experiences of the games. We streamed in, angelic beings with all our different qualities and capabilities ready to be used. We swirled into space and began to set up systems comprised mainly of stars and planets; although there is much more than these alive in this universe. We negotiated with the dark angels present to set ground rules for the games. Had we done this before? Yes, many times going back into timelessness. The centre where the Creator's light shines is a timeless area; and a universe incorporating laws of linear time and space is different for us. There appears to be a past, present and future, but there is always only now.

Where did the angels all come from? In the beginning we came from outside this universe and were formed of the Creator, who created us out of love and the wholeness and vastness of its being. We were born as aspects of the Creator itself and each of us angels represents a quality that is present in the Creator. We are more than a single quality however, we are also whole, but in this game we are representing aspects of the Creator. We have roles to play to make this game go forward in the manner it was designed, to be team leaders each with our own teams standing behind us. In this game some are light, and some are dark, and many are neither. We entered into the universes for the games to begin. The dark angels are as much a part of God as are the angels of light. Having said that, in this universe, in this game they are our adversaries; our roles are to contest with each other at all times for the end result. The end result we desire is joy and bliss, we are attuned to these vibrations ourselves and value them above all others. The other side offers the direct opposite: misery and suffering.

The Creator has a dark side? The Creator of us all contains everything there is, light and dark. All is present in the Creator, he is *whole*. I also contain light and dark, but it is my role to personify light and hold that for the angels of light, for I am light itself, the Archangel of Light. This means I show you only one side of myself during this game, and I devote myself to the light, love and truth. For truth does not hide in the darkness. During this game I have worked hard to bring light to every corner of the universe, just as my adversary has sought to bring darkness.

This universe has hung in the balance for a long time between the light and the dark. It is time now for this planet to tip the balance for one or the other. As this planet goes, so goes the universe. It is not normal for a planet's rise into light or descent into darkness to affect the whole universe, but such is the state of balance at this time.

So we meet each other and contest with each other on every planet, and through the spaces in between. Our remit is to help all souls reach their fullest potential; to explore the limits of darkness and the limits of light; as this is the nature of this game. This game explores the limitations of light and dark; what happens when they have been split and set against each other? What results arise from such a division, and what does God learn about his own nature from this? Much has been learned here that could not have been learned in a timeless universe. If you liken God to a large and colourful woven tapestry, we are all the different threads that make up the whole. That tapestry has dissolved itself to play this game inside this universe. You must remember that you humans are threads within the tapestry also and you are engaged in learning about what it is to be God. God comprises everything in this universe; God is literally All That Is. When you think of God, look in the mirror; for you are a tiny example of the wholeness of God. And remember, each soul group runs the risk of incarnating for a game and living their lives out in misery. Caught in the web of darkness these souls live in darkness, and work with the dark angels to foster hell.

Where is hell? Hell is here, you live in a hell created with the vibrations of fear, misery, loathing, violence and contempt. This planet did not always host hell; in the previous soul groups hell never really took hold. The early ages of Atlantis were not like this, although there were pockets of darkness present from the very beginning. The pockets of darkness were dangerous to the first humans who were beginning their game. They lay across the land where they could most easily interfere with the human game players. The humans could not see these pockets and did not know they were present. This was part of the means by which the downfall of Atlantis was brought about. By the fourth age of Atlantis there was a shift very quickly towards the dark.

Now that so much time has elapsed we must conclude that the dark was inherent in the rules of the game that were laid out in the contract between the planet and the humans. The loneliness and isolation were root causes of unhappiness, these led into misery more easily than we foresaw. The game was predisposed to misery, to the dark. We wanted to appear to you, to support you and let you know that you were not alone and bring you the light of connection, but the upper dimensions were veiled from you.

As angels of light we broadcast love onto this planet, and showered it with joy. We came with swords of love and fought the angels of the darkness to protect you from them. We incarnated ourselves here to live lives of light and instruction; but it was never easy for us to live here and got harder and harder as time went by. We found those who would listen to us; who were able to hear and understand us and gave our messages of hope and love and reminders of God and his all-encompassing nature. Often these prophets of ours were the founders of religions; founded by some of their followers who clung to the mistaken notion that the prophet was more than a mouthpiece for something greater. Those who wished to follow the teachings of the prophets never understood their own place as a tiny part of All That Is. The teachings of our prophets added to the multitude of religions in the world. All these different religions were founded with the same goal, to understand the nature of God and of their own lives and purpose in living. The human soul splintered here longed for the warmth of joy and connection in their lonely lives.

All the time the planet darkened, bit by bit. In the shadows of Atlantis there were demon breeding grounds, the first time we had witnessed this here. And it was Earth, the shining one, who was being damaged in this way! It is extremely dangerous for humans to live with higher dimensional demons breeding among them unseen. Only on this planet were the higher dimensions veiled, invisible and inaudible. But they can see and hear you and have listeners who keep watch over you to make sure you are not detecting their presence. Humans who are able to see slightly through the dimensional veils are at risk from interaction with these and need to exercise caution. This means asking us for help and protection, and paying attention to their security arrangements. Few humans are powerful enough or well protected enough to fight them off alone. They will attack and destroy those who get in their way; some of you know what I'm talking about. From time to time you have had visionaries and those who were able to see figures and receive messages from the higher dimensions. Led by your institutions of religion these people were usually killed as the messages they brought were not in line with the teachings of these authorities. Your religions remind us of wolves with the main object of controlling and eating the flocks of sheep with plenty of rewards for those in charge.

The humans lived side by side with those who sought to turn their lives into painful misery. As these demons increased their numbers the pockets of darkness swarmed as a pit of snakes would swarm, and those humans who carelessly walked across them would be tainted. Beware of the ground under your feet and don't walk places that *feel* bad, as there is only one reason why the Earth would feel unsafe to you. When this happens there is seldom an effort made to dislodge the dark; why would there be if no one can see it is there? These areas are still found in some places on your planet, and they are not easy to see. The original game plan veiled the higher dimensions from the players, and these pockets are in the higher dimensions. The humans had allowed this dangerous element to be inserted into the original plan by the dark angels.

When I talk about dark angels breeding, what do I mean exactly? How do dark angels breed? How do their numbers increase, and does the number of light angels also increase? The dark angels were able to increase their numbers in any area they had enough food. They bred not as humans breed now, with two people coming together, but by having enough energy to divide and increase their numbers. In the dark places of the universe there are an ever-increasing number of dark entities who devote their energies to multiplying their numbers. It is within their rights as part of their role; however it makes it less easy for us.

We, on the other hand focus the light of the stars onto the various life forms on the different worlds, we increase the brightness of the communities there, and allow the light to increase in that manner. We seek to cover the universe in light or dark by different means. The universe is in a state of precarious balance now, and that partly explains the great interest in the outcome here. As this planet tips towards darkness the dark angels can see their energy flowing out like a river extinguishing the stars.

Angels have many functions; both dark and light. The functions of angels in this universe are restricted; we have chosen our roles and we do not waver. And each kind of angel has their polar opposite in function, if not in form. In other words, where there are the mighty angels of light: Elohim, Principalities, Mentalities, Seraphim, and Cherubim collectives there are the corresponding dark collectives. The great archangels known to humans have their dark counterparts and the numbers of smaller angels are many, as are the smaller entities of darkness. I have implied that some angels are greater than others, this is not so. We are all a part of the One who created us, none is greater than another. We all have different functions and roles. The role of the archangels involves teaching humans on this planet, therefore humans gave them a name with the prefix 'arch' but we do not recognise ourselves as higher than any of the other angels, light or dark. The title Archangel we will continue to use as long as it is in common human use and contributes to making our information clearer. One day we would like to provide you with a detailed book on angels through this channel so that you can know our variety and kinds. There is other, more time sensitive material to send through first. We angels of light are the same as far as our natures go, we are light, we are love, we are music and joy. When you think of us, remember us for what we are; that expression of the nature of God present in all those things, and more. We stand beside you as you walk through your lives on this planet and we hear you when you speak to us and ask us for help.

2

IN THE BEGINNING we were formed from the desire of the Creator to explore his own nature, out of the Creator's wish to examine the threads more closely, to see the colours more brightly and to know in greater detail what it is to be God. We emerged as angels, and then we divided with the light going one way and the dark the other, the choice was ours to make. We were complete as individuals because we knew who we were and where we came from. Our purposes were made clear to us as we examined our own roles, and we helped prepare the new universe for the exploration of limitation; of time and of polarisation. Into this new universe, and the many others that were set up at that time all playing the same game, we came with our co-workers, among whom are the stars of light that shine with all of our angelic qualities. The stars radiated out love, life, joy and song. When you credit your local sun with providing the energy for life on your planet of course you are right, that is one of the primary functions of all stars. The stars in the heavens are our allies in light; bringers of the light to open up the dark spaces where fear, lies and other manifestations of darkness can hide. These stars are beings who are the part of the Creator that is light, and they have taken this form to shine light and life into this universe. They are faithful and true, and we value them for their steadfast service during the long ages of the universe.

In the beginning we maintained our light through and around the stars, to make it available for all planetary life in the universe. Stars produce light and life for the dark as well as the light beings that live here. Your planet relies on the light of your sun, and the darkness has been gathering here on Earth for a long, long time. The function of light is also to give a place where truth can be seen, where there is no place for lies to hide. On your planet the absence of truth is universal and expected. You expect your governments and others to lie to you, because you know that they lie constantly for their own protection and self-gain. You discount all that you see and hear because it may not be true. When all is lit and out in the open these lies have nowhere to hide and multiply, they cannot exist in the light of truth. Light has so many meanings. When you choose to live in the light you are able to carry with you the discernment to shine light on subjects that have been woven in darkness to deceive you. The light chases shadows from the corners of the room where the dark is used to working. The dark side does not wish you to know of your ability to do this, to see into the darkness with your own shining qualities of light. You humans have the ability use light to see with your hearts and head where the darkness lies; and who is telling the truth and who is twisting words into lies. You are not using your ability to discern frequently enough. Try it and see how easy it is to be a human lie-detector by using your discernment.

Where the light of the stars does not reach (and you can picture to yourselves the dark in between the stars) then beware; this is an area under control of the dark angels. What occurs there is hidden from you, although not from us. These areas of darkness between the galaxies are not safe for you to enter into. Absence of light escaping does not mean there is no light there at all, but there is very little remaining between the large galactic star families. Some parts of the universe are covered in impenetrable, dark, thick fog impossible for you to see through. We go there at our peril as the fighting is intense between us at all times. There are dark planets of pain and misery; whole systems that we are barred from by the numbers of dark angels present there. The lives lived there have slid into complete and utter darkness. These are lives of emptiness, of fear and self-loathing. Those who live in such parts of the universe express sorrow in every fibre of their beings. There is no vibrancy and joy of life, no love or music or laughter. Instead there is weeping and grief and they are surrounded by the deaths and annihilation of their families. This is not altogether unfamiliar to you. We are able to provide light to them in the form of distant stars from far off galaxies. On these planets all is hidden in lies and darkness, and the lives are lived in slavery to fear and misery. War succeeds war, and a painful death occurring in fearful circumstances is all they know. We see them and we pity them. All lessons learned on these planets are of value to the Creator.

These areas of darkness do not have stars that give life; they have beings that live on the pain and misery of those living on the planet. These planets are dying and the races that live on them do not even know or care. The lives of the planets have been sacrificed needlessly as planets are happy to live with the races playing the game. These planets have been smothered and prevented from receiving from the universe the sustenance and energy they need to live. They have been prevented from receiving the flow of universal life force energy that is their connection to All That Is. There is no greater sorrow to us than the death of a planet during a game they contracted to play. This is how the dark angels feed; they are our opposite, where we give life through light they live on the life that exists elsewhere and take from them. Learn what darkness looks like and stop being fooled by those who would take everything from you. You have the power to stop them.

Where these areas of the universe are in darkness we are seldom able to visit now in force. We concentrate our greatest efforts on the planets where both light and dark are present; trying to sway the planet to the light. Now our main focus at this time is on your planet. Earth is a classic example of one of these planets in many ways. There is still some light on your planet, and you are not very close to the powerful central suns of your galaxy where the light shines the brightest. Your planet has the greatest concentration of angels of light and dark of any planet in this universe at this time.

This area of your galaxy is relatively quiet, and your neighbouring planets are united with you in your goals. There is nothing to fear from your local solar system. The closest stars have some advanced-level games in progress and know enough to stay away from Earth. There are alien visitors to your planet, but at such low levels as to be almost non-existent. They are not blinded to the upper dimensions and have little wish to approach here; a planet swarming with demons of all shapes and sizes. They are not a problem yet and we are keeping such visitors well away. We do not need another planet's life forms landing here and do not permit their passage through your solar system. The real dark empires of this universe are far enough away that they are not a pressing problem at this time. And yet darkness spreads out from this planet, reaching out to touch the nearest planets and stars. The darkness is greatest in the higher dimensions where the real decisions are made about what happens here on Earth. They are easily visible from space when looking here, and their damage to your planet can be seen by all but you. Your nearest planet neighbours are alarmed and concerned. They have their shields up at full strength and are trusting in their own light and help from us to keep them safe. This solar system has always stood by Earth and cherished her as the shining one, the one who had hosted successful games where much was learned.

The dark that began with the inherent loneliness of this game allowed this planet to become covered with the kind of thick, tarry darkness that is the precursor to the entire planet becoming dark all the way through to the core. This planet actively resisted this and the crystals imbedded throughout her structure aided her in a conscious way. They were the other soul group here, and they put their efforts into resisting the dark.

Humans meanwhile had come to the beginning of the end days of Atlantis.

3

THERE CAME A TIME in Atlantis when the dark that had lain in pools across the surface of the Earth became attached to enough incarnate humans to influence their behaviour. Their behaviour began to further separate each human from one another as each lived lives devoted to their own self and ceased to regard others. Demons you call them, when they attach themselves to people and take them over in this way. As there is no love in the demons they do not act in the interest of the human host, but only in their own interest. This is important to remember as there are humans now who have one or more of these demons attached to them dictating their behaviour and who feel that they are able to gain something by hosting demons; but they are only used and discarded. Humans have such short lives now that the host body has a rapid turnover. These demons go from human to human to human and spend many of your lives here in places they can do the most damage. Where you see those whose actions are very harmful then you know that the controller is an entity of darkness.

When a human is controlled by the dark their actions begin to harm others in many ways. You begin to hear ideas from them that bear no resemblance to love: love for themselves, others, the planet, and all that live here by the grace of God. This is where I would like to point the finger at the world religions, and I know that if I give examples from one religion others may feel that their religion avoids these pitfalls. No religion avoids these pitfalls. One thing that all religions have in common is their insistence that if their rules are obeyed, then the follower will somehow come closer to God. There is no rule to coming closer to God and all these religions have found a way to keep you separated from God. We look at all of them, I repeat: all of them, and see the darkest clouds of hate on this planet.

There were many instances of hatred stirred up against fellow human beings by religion in the last century. That one century saw Hindus and Muslims murdering each other in the partition of India, and Jews, Muslims and Christians killing their neighbours in Palestine and

Northern Ireland, to give just three examples out of many. People are living in fear of each other and preparing to stand up to each other and say God can only be found following their religion's rules. Where is the love of God present in any of this? God is love, overwhelming, encompassing love for each and every thing he has created. We can see all those dark entities that are controlling these world religions, and more and more there are humans who are able to see them also. Beware of the message and the messenger.

In the days of Atlantis there were no religions. The temples of the Archangels had nothing to do with religious worship; they were places of healing and connection to the outer universe. The wooden temples of the archangels were removed by those who desired to remove our influence, and were 'improved' as temples of stone. This had the effect of making us seem more distant from the Atlanteans; previously we were seen as helpers, not semi-divine. It was harder to feel our love in a building made of stone. The new temples of Atlantis were cold and grand and our own priests and priestesses began to feel they were more important than they really were. They assumed an air of privilege where previously they had been approachable healers. The size and richness of the new buildings implied that the Archangels were grander than the ones who were coming there to be in contact with them.

Once this artificial division had begun, and had seeped into the consciousness of the Atlanteans it became very difficult for us to be heard as we wished to be, with our own priests controlling what could and could not be said and done. The head priests no longer went to the healing tables themselves. An undercurrent of contempt for those who came to be healed began to show. The priests of the archangels began to be arrogant about their roles, and about their knowledge and abilities. Rules began to be introduced that governed temple use. Where before a person could come and just sit in the garden they were now prevented from casual visits. When the role of teacher came to be considered better than the role of student it started a process of separation. The people's belief that the angels were better than they were led them to wrongly believe that they were unworthy of being part of God. They were not good enough to stand as an independent particle of the Creator of all. Up until this time they had been able to see that they were not separate from God, that they themselves were God, made out of God in an effort to learn more about All That Is. It's as if God said 'I will divide myself into pieces and play these new games and learn as much as I can about my own nature.'

God lives inside of you; and outside of you in everything in this universe. When you believe God is a far off master of the universe you are not entirely right, that far off God *is* this universe. He is the Creator of everything here, large and small, which exists in this entire universe you live in. You actually are the God who created everything. But you feel very small and have forgotten that you are one and the same as the Creator. This forgetting began when the temples stopped being made out of trees. The trees are still here on your planet and you can still be helped by being with them outdoors in the countryside. These are not our temples, but they are still good places to connect to God.

When our temples of wood were removed we found an alteration in the people coming to the stone temples and a falling-off in the numbers visiting. Instead of acting on behalf of the planet, people sought to have the healing done to them, for them. This was not a good sign as previously the population had understood how to remain healthy by connecting through their own self-treatment of Reiki daily. Now we looked to see if the self-treatments were regular in the people coming to the temples and they were not. Nor were they regular in joining the large healing circles in the villages. They required the temple healers to give them special attention and treatments. As the Fourth Age progressed the healers in the temples regularly treated patients all day, although this was unknown in the previous ages. Those who were treated by the priests regained health for the most part. There came a time when the temples became quiet and very few came for healing any more. After that came the actions that led to the downfall of Atlantis.

I speak about the temples as if they were the cause of the destruction of Atlantis, but they were a symptom of the change in the people of Atlantis. The Atlanteans had left behind a respect for their land and moved into large cities where they were no longer nourished by contact with planet Earth all day. These city dwellers began to show signs of imbalance and derangement in our view; it was as if we were watching people deliberately seeking to be made ill. As they progressed in their lack of connection to their planet, and only visiting the countryside on special occasions; we saw them sink into fascination with what we would call dark arts, and you would call scientific experiments. Not all of your scientific experimentation are worthy of undertaking, and if these experiments were openly done and understood by you today you would stop a great many of them from progressing. Science began to be all-consuming to these later Atlanteans and it was felt that science would lead them into greater and greater civilisation and progress. As you discuss the latest movies and music, they discussed the latest scientific experiments and breakthroughs at social get-togethers. They transferred their respect from the planet and other living animals and plants and gave it to science.

We saw the falling-off of the Reiki self-treatment and the communal healing circles as the greatest blow against the light on Earth. It is not possible to be kept whole and healthy by relying on someone other than yourself. The planet could not be kept whole and healthy without being provided with Reiki. Allowing themselves to believe that everything would still be fine, that someone else would take care of them and the planet was enough to allow the dark to tip the balance, cover the planet completely with tar and begin to take this soul group down into blackness. Once they could cover a planet in tar that was usually the signal for the planet's suffocation.

We watched as the horrors of Atlantis in the Fourth Age manifested. I am prepared to talk about these in some detail as much of this is being repeated now, and much that was rejected as being too foul then is present in your world today. Atlantis holds many lessons for you now as you enter into new scientific procedures that are old, Atlantean technology. You have manipulated your plant's genes to create new crops. These crops are combinations of plant and animal life and are a huge mistake. This is not a path that will benefit anyone on your planet except the ones holding the patents and controlling the crops. The GM crops will be directly linked to future famines. You are also draining all of your oil and coal reserves as quickly as you can. The Atlanteans used crystal energy provided by the Earth, but in the end they abused that source of power. The oil industry is one of the unkindest industries you have ever unleashed onto the planet. It removes a substance from the Earth that she uses for her own needs, her own flow and circulation, and burns it up, removing it forever. The industry and the oil burning combine to spoil the surface and atmosphere of the Earth. There are many ways of degrading humans and the planet. Look for those who have the most to gain from all this destruction to know who is controlled by the dark. There are many, many of them in your world governments and religions. By their actions you will recognise them.

Atlanteans in the Fourth Age built a machine that allowed the separation of the androgynous human soul into two halves, male and female. This was a great novelty, and one person could look into their own eyes and see half of their characteristics reflected back to them in another living person. They would go about in pairs, and became inseparable from each other, but they were separate people now. They were neither of them balanced any longer and clung to each other in an attempt to maintain a whole sense of their original self. But as these halves died eventually, with a much shorter lifespan than previously, there was no putting back what had been split apart.

When these half-souls came to reincarnate again they could chose male or female. Souls still have this choice. Reincarnated souls following the division searched for their original missing half during their lifetimes, but this is very hard when wearing a veil. Sometimes they are found for a lifetime, and other times they partner another half-soul and finish out a life with some sense of balance. Their search for their other half blinds them to their original purpose of their lives here, to discover God; not their perfect partner or soul-mate.

Time passed and it was like watching a species deranged. The equilibrium they had gained in previous ages was gone. The search for their soul-mate was an obsession, but these were now reincarnating so randomly that there was little chance of meeting and spending a life together. In death there was despair, their brief time above the planet in the waiting area was their only chance to be free of the pain of separation. In life and death their unhappiness grew. When their bodies aged they resisted death remaining alive in a feeble state. If only they could live longer, they might find themselves and reunite for a little time and be whole again. This was when the cloning began.

The cloning was an attempt to stay alive at all times, a refusal to let the body die and stay young. You may have read about humans being cloned for spare body parts, but do you know what that did to the existing souls? There were versions of themselves alive for spare parts, but their soul was also in them, not duplicated but divided. The original that had clones made did not see that their own soul had to divide and leave their body to give life to the new body being created. To us this was a further splintering of souls. Where the last element of the game had led to souls being cut in half, some now had many clones, many divisions. This did not allow for the reflection on the experiences of the soul that takes place when the soul is not incarnate, as the soul was now continually present on Earth in at least one body. They had achieved a degree of physical longevity through their use of clones, but their very souls were under strain. The human soul that had designed and requested this game was vanishing into ever smaller and smaller pieces; and these little pieces were blind, deaf and dumb to what was happening to them.

As they fell away into this darkness of ever searching for their undivided soul, the balance of the planet tipped. The Earth could not maintain her equilibrium or position as a planet of light when this was happening on her surface. She could not be free and independent of the darkness smothering her, and the energy of the game was now very destructive and filled with hatred. From this time on the game was played without her co-operation as she realised that her own life was at risk. The humans were now her enemy and her bounty towards them was withdrawn. They could live on her if they liked, but she didn't have to make it easy for them. Some of the things you are familiar with began to happen: drought, floods, earthquakes and volcanoes. Until you as a species resume your responsibilities towards her you will not see her as she can be; the bounteous giver of life. She has her own life and well-being to consider. Remember this: the answer to your global warming is in your own hands.

As babies these humans were now, but like permanent babies who had no way to learn or grow into their next step of development. Some were in positions of power over their fellow men and their animals and they began to seriously abuse that power. The clones would murder each other in order to obtain replacements for their worn out body parts, not realising that the human clone in front of them was as alive as they themselves were. Or sometimes the one that survived was the more recent clone with the same face, body and soul of the older person. The value and respect they had for one another in their lives, as living beings that each had a right to belong on the planet was fast ebbing away. The situation in Atlantis was one of destruction and evil. When you contemplate cannibalism today you think of something abhorrent, of men eating other men. This was men growing other men for harvest of their body parts and subsequent death. It was destroying the society and lives of the Atlanteans themselves, even though they were hanging onto their physical lives. When we had watched them go past the point of no return, when our temples were destroyed and the Earth seen as a captive source of plunder instead of a respected giver of her own body as a home, then we acted.

Angels can act when there is need. We do not do this lightly, but sometimes what is happening is so sickening and evil that we make arrangements and step in to prevent worse from happening. These last days of Atlantis were so destructive to the planet herself, not to mention the humans that we made our plans and intervened. When the time came to act, when the last warnings had gone unheeded, we removed the land itself from the physical dimensions. The island of Atlantis is still there in the higher dimensions as it belongs to the Earth and not us, but on the physical plane the land was wrenched away. Where there was land before, there was now just the sea, washing over the place the land had been. The tsunami caused by the removal of the island was large enough to affect the surrounding land masses and sink ships. A great hole was ripped through the layers of the upper dimensions, a wound that has not yet healed. It was a severe way of solving a problem, and one we did not undertake lightly.

This wrenching away of the island of Atlantis was possible once we got permission to act on behalf of the Earth. We are not allowed to enter into games and change them because we feel that we could improve the games, or influence the games to come out as we wish them too. So many times in the past we have had to stand by and watch while whole planets turned their backs to the light and slid into darkness. There are times now when we have had to stand by and watch individual actions on this planet and were not allowed to step in. We often wish we could. This particular time was approved by the Creator of us all, in the sense of unified action. The planet itself had asked us for help, and there were still people in Atlantis who asked for our help. Off planet there were worried observers from other local planets that were concerned. The darkness coming from this area was a spewing out of foul energy that threatened this solar system. There was not enough light here to balance the darkness of this civilisation.

Surely other planets had worse things going on? There are many other planets of darkness where choices have been made to enslave and torment others, but they were working as a unified consciousness. The enslavement and torment was directed at other group souls, and although there was nothing good about this, the horror that was Atlantis was unique: a soul tearing itself apart, devouring itself. We did not have the power or desire to end the game, but we wanted to wipe the slate clean and see them start over. This we were able to do.

Those who escaped to establish their new homes in Africa, America, Europe and Asia did not have the crystal power to continue with their comfortable lives. The crystals had withdrawn their power from the humans as it had facilitated their scientific experiments. In the final days the scientists turned to experiments on the living crystals. Could they pierce their hearts and funnel dark energy into them and change their nature? This act of manipulation to turn light into dark, to foul these life forms through attack and poison caused the deaths of these captive crystals. Before this black energy could flow into the rest of the crystals and from them into the planet, these dying crystals were cut off and died in agony. It is painful to remember and write about. They chose to withdraw completely and utterly. When you meet a crystal now, they sit silently for the most part and pretend to be little more than pretty rocks. They will work with you if they trust you, if they can see your own inner light shining. There is a limit to what one life form will undergo for another.

The remnants of the Atlantean cultures are gone from this planet now. When you meet with cloning you are coming to it freshly; it has been completely rediscovered by your modern scientists. This is an abomination and is promoted by those who have no concept of their own souls. You are being told what is right, wrong, and acceptable by those who have no idea. Their focus is on the minutia and detail of scientific experiments, not on what is appropriate or morally right. Beware of the soulless scientists and their justifications of perverted research. In their dogmatic pursuit of their fields of interest, and in their ruthless methods of testing they have left the moral high-ground behind. It is not all about money! The good that can come from these experiments involving human health is very little compared to the time and money spent looking in the wrong direction. The healing of the physical body is about connection to the universal life force energy and all that that brings to the person and planet.

4

THE DAMAGE DONE to the Earth by the Atlanteans began when they chose to use the crystal energy to make their experiments possible. The cloning experiments were only the last in a long line of destructive and disrespectful acts against the totality of life on and including the planet. Cloning was the final step that sealed the fate of Atlantis.

The damaged crystals were removed when the continent was wrenched away, and they were able to leave the physical shell behind and join into their mass consciousness. No crystal lives were lost in that way.

Many and varied were the crystals of Atlantis. In addition to the generator crystals were the light-giving crystals used in the homes and other buildings. These crystals used the Earth's energy to provide light from within. There is another type I would mention, the communicating crystals used for long distance communication between villages. People kept in touch with the central communicating crystals, and this service was provided to promote some cohesion to the human race. The communicating crystals were able to pulse the information over long distances and were rather taken for granted. You are beginning to employ crystals again for communication in your computers and mobile phones. They are perfect for facilitating communication, but in the past all you needed was the crystals, and their energy was of life itself not of harmful wavelengths.

The Atlantean communication crystals are still talked about today as one of the wonders of Atlantis. These crystals opened a pathway through to the consciousness of the Earth so that there could be a partnership between the humans and the planet. Up until the fourth age the planet was allowed to be consulted as to her needs, and there was a dialogue between humans and planet. These crystals were first neglected, and then withdrew themselves from service. When the last one was gone the Earth was shut off from the humans and all forms of sentient conversation with them ceased. These crystals are now waiting to re-emerge from the depths they travelled to when escaping the destruction of Atlantis. They have been working their way towards the surface and will come through at the right time, in the right places to resume their old roles.

Crystals are woven through the Atlantean history from the beginning to the end. It was they who worked with us on behalf of the planet; and they are still here on her behalf. The planet is home to the crystal kingdoms and they have dedicated themselves to her protection. All who help and serve the planet will find their efforts and journeys easier if they include crystals in their daily lives. Crystals are prepared to help those who accept that they have much to give and are ready to align themselves with them and the planet Earth.

5

I AM THE ANGEL of Light, and it is my task in this book to teach you about my counterpart, the Angel of Dark. I have spent my long ages with Melchizadek and others in the preservation of the light here, and it is my purpose to see this universe end in light: in love, joy and laughter.

The role of the light is to cultivate and cherish joy and love, to increase their presence and see them spread ever wider. On your planet you have farmers who plant seeds and help them to grow by weeding out smothering weeds and protecting the young plants from birds and dry weather. I am such a farmer, and I seed love and joy into all worlds I can reach, and encourage them to grow into bliss and happiness, and wholeness of body and spirit. When the dark comes to smother we come with swords to contest for the young expressions of light, and fight to protect all that there is, no matter where it is to be found, that is light.

When the dark takes hold and substitutes its own qualities of misery, hatred and violence among others, I am still there fighting for the light. This struggle has been going on so long now, as long as the universe itself has existed. On planet after planet battles have been fought and won or lost to the dark. Where they have been lost those worlds have sunk into misery and the planets themselves are deeply damaged or as good as dead. This planet has been under serious attack for a long time now, and we have been fighting a guerrilla war against the dominant dark force. The dark force on this planet is religion. The most successful tool for defeating the light has for a long time been the various religions. Long ago these religions lost their way in leading their followers to God. I am speaking here of the religions who tell their followers how to reach God through living in certain ways and following rules of behaviour. Following rules that were created by those who wished to exercise power over others by dictating how they were to live is one of this planets great sadnesses . Do you think we will stand here and do nothing while religions slaughter their own followers by sending them against one another? We do not blame the followers so much as the leaders who have deceived them.

The time has come to end religion on this planet, and end the control of the religions by the dark angels. They are a breeding ground for the emotions of fear, hatred, guilt, anger, intolerance and violence. Our plans are now made and you will see them all crashing down in the next few years. Some of you who read this book will be the ones to walk away from them, and without followers their power will cease. Without them driving their followers forward into violence there will be a great lessening of the killing and wars here.

The end of these world religions will come suddenly, and soon. When they cease their manipulations of you who are human, you will wake up and see that you are not bad and sinful, and unworthy of love by your God, you will see that you were tricked. You will see that they kept you far away from God, and that you knew God personally all the time. All they did was to make sure you could not reach your Creator through the wall they convinced you was there. You will think of your religious leaders and say, not that kind and good man or woman. Your religious leaders sought to lead you to God, but they were themselves mislead by the dark angels who inserted into your religion the fear and hatred that is found in all your religions. Your fear and hatred of all who search by different spiritual paths than the one you are on.

Religions established on this planet have been used as a way to differentiate tribal groups from each other. You are able to tell who is similar to yourself if they practise religion in the same manner that you do. You may all originally come from the same part of the globe. You want to know who is like you, or "one of us", and who isn't. What religion does not give you is how you are all the same, how very small your differences are between one human and another. Religion has been used to divide you from each other and keep you fighting. You can not join together and learn about yourselves in peace if you are busy attacking and defending yourselves. Why would you want to learn about yourselves? Because the Creator made this universe to learn about itself; and separated into many pieces to play games and have experiences. Each piece of the Creator in this universe has the same capabilities as the one who began the game. You do not use your abilities to create because you are not taught that you are born able to do this. So you create very little, and much of it is guided by your religions into creating unhappiness.

6

THE TIME HAS come to look closely at these religions and truly consider them for what they are. They all have some characteristics in common; the most common one is to say that if you follow my rules, which are the only correct rules, you will find that during this life or after you die, you will come to a good place. All have something positive to gain from following their rules, and all the other religions' rules are false. Only by following the rules of your own religion is it possible to have the desired result. The followers of all other religions are deluded and will have no reward at the end of their lives because they lived by a set of rules that led nowhere. And as for drawing closer to their own version of God, they see this as a by-product of living by the rules.

This just sounds pointless and misguided until you find the undercurrent of contempt and hatred that each has for the other. Even within the same religion, as in the sects of Christianity where there is killing in Northern Ireland; and in the fighting between the branches of Islam in the war-torn countries of the Middle East. The castes of Hinduism are contemptuous of the castes lower than themselves. There is disagreement in Judaism on following an intricate set of rules the most faithfully. The four main religions are but examples representative of the many smaller religions in the world. I let none of them off the hook, they all serve the same purpose and that is to create a distance between yourselves and God. There is *no distance* between yourselves and God, as you contain God inside you. Prayers addressed to a far-off God in heaven are pointing the wrong way. Look into your hearts and you will find God; and that God is the one who will answer all of your prayers with wisdom and love.

How angry these words will make many people, I know. There has been so much invested in worshipping a far away God, and following the rules necessary to reach that God. It is as if you are trying to build a ladder to the farthest star by using a set of rules that never made any sense to start with. You don't have to believe impossible things to find God, or achieve endless good works. There is no division between you and God; so you don't need to acknowledge another human as being necessary to show you how to find God. There is nothing you have to learn to find God, nothing you have to do; you can't be separated from God – you are God.

So if you're God, why don't you know this and get busy being God? You actually are busy being God, and you created your life in this world, and you created this game and world to live on. The Earth was a creation of God along side of you in the beginning and she is able to also create for herself. So how does all of this fit together, it seems as if there should be billions of different Earths here right now, maybe each with only one human on it? The creating you are doing is a result of the one human unified soul, and the Earth is a unified soul and you have a contract. On the day to day creation front most of you have no idea what you are creating. You create haphazardly, and unless you believe me, or know by previous experience the possibility of creating seriously from scratch you will not be creating anything differently from your neighbours. You each have the power to choose and live the life you desire. There will be more about this in the final chapters. But some of you know, and some of you are busy creating, stepping into the knowledge you are God and changing your lives and the life of this planet in a good way. Do you want a clue as to who these people are? Look for those who are expressing joy in their lives. They are walking free in the knowledge they are God, and they are joyful in that knowledge for they have rejoined themselves to their Creator and are no longer alone.

Do you want to learn more about yourself to understand yourself as God? Do you want to find some help somewhere so that you can come closer to this part of yourself that is unfamiliar to you, and perhaps create joy? Ask for help, ask angels for help, and we will come and help you. If you trust us to give you life experiences to show you more about yourself as God, ask us to provide them. Others may successfully ask for visions or messages, it depends on you. Maybe that will be the first thing you create, the ability to see or hear from the higher dimensions. Angels come from the spiritual heart of the Creator and we are able to help you in spiritual ways. If you wish to create earthly treasures, you may work on that one also, but we will not give you a pot of gold. You will give yourself a pot of gold.

Creating is a function of the Creator, and when you stepped down on this planet as blank pieces of paper long ago you began a game to find the central part of yourself that is the Creator. Although you are now here living this game, all lives on all planets are also the Creator playing their games. The Creator is a unified whole, and is separate across the universe in All That Is. The Creator is here in this universe, is outside this universe, and in other universes. It was not part of your game to remember this about yourselves or your God, or to remember that there is a God at all. And yet we watched the most blind, helpless species you could ever imagine continue to find God. Not all of you chose to find God, but so many of you did in every age and circumstance, and with no idea of what you were doing when you began to search. It has been extraordinary and scary at the same time. But now we are ready to help the humans gather together and become one again, in preparation for the times that are coming and the ending of the contract.

7

THIS CONTRACT WILL end when all humans willingly rejoin together again as one. That day is still many lifetimes away, but there are some key events that will take place soon, and the first one is in the year 2012. At that time the crystal energy will resurface and reconnect to the universe. There will follow many years of adjustments when there will be quite dramatic changes taking place. These changes will affect both the human race and the planet, and the changes will broadcast outwards to incrementally change the universe also as nothing exists in isolation. When these changes begin they will begin slowly and speed up as everyone adapts.

First let me talk about the years before 2012, when there will be troubled times, and dangerous times. There are those who will see this book and other information from other sources as threatening to their power base and income. Without warning there will be deaths between those who each follow their own religions and those who they see as opposing them. Without the realisation that they are killing their own other-selves, lives will be taken in the name of religion until the rest of humanity is so sickened by it that they withdraw from supporting any religion at all. These will be painful days but they will not last long. The human race is ready to give up following religions and turn away from them and back to the light. When enough have rejected religion there will be too few left to continue the killing, and nowhere to recruit from. There will be no more hiding behind a false front of a manufactured God. This will mark a new beginning for the players of the game, and the final phase will get underway. There is no room for religion and its divisive effects in the final phase.

The final phase will last many lifetimes, but each succeeding generation will know their own worth as a Creator to a greater and greater degree. And they will create those things that have value and worth: peace and joy; love and hope. There will be a greater connection between each living human with one another. This will allow for the redevelopment of telepathy so that there will be greater understanding between you. The group mind that is similar to the one present in the animal species on your planet will be the final development. When all is known and understood and shared, and the human soul sees its unity and its place as an expression of God in this universe, the game will be over and the contract ended. What follows after that will be a joining of this soul to the other souls of light in active battle against the dark for the ultimate outcome of this overarching game: that the whole universe joins the light before the time comes to return to the Creator. There are other universes to balance out that will have descended into darkness.

This universe still has a long way to go until the end.

8

A LONG TIME AGO, before this manufacture of religions ever began, people related to each other by connecting through their hearts. When they connected through their hearts with love to each other they could not believe that God was absent from their daily life. There was an open channel of love connecting them to all others of their own kind and they found kindness and love at the hands of all whether family or strangers. They could look into the eyes of another human and see that there was a soul inside that was as worthy of respect as they were themselves. The separation of the human soul into unknowing fragments did not mean that they could not recognise that others were also human and of value. This recognition of self inside another would have been enough to start all humanity onto a path to end the game successfully.

The catastrophe of one human denying the humanity of another was brought about through the interference of our dark angelic brethren, and serves their purpose of creating misery. The point of view took hold that others were "not us", and inferior to "us" and it was done to emphasise that they were special and chosen, and were being loyal to their God in the only correct way. That this was manufactured by themselves as walls and barriers to keep them further apart did not occur to them. All these religions are committed to believing that they are the only ones living by the correct rules. Interestingly, they also had to manufacture a God that was content to see them behave by the rules they had drawn up. I have to hand it to the dark angels for coming up with an inspired and effective method of dividing humanity and keeping them from finding their Creator.

As time went on and these religions took greater and greater hold on their respective captive populations, they formed an incredible backdrop to world wars. The incessant "God supports my side" has been present for thousands of years. You are still having these religious wars, where the loving God supports you in killing someone you disagree with. As I watch this being replayed over and over again I feel sorrow to the depths of my being.

At this time your religions are causing more pain and death than from any other cause on the planet by far. It has been this way for many centuries, and continues now in a bloodbath of hatred. All your religious tracts were inspired by prophets who had a message to try to get everyone to turn and find God in their hearts and lives. Very few of the followers of the modern religions have come anywhere near finding God in their hearts. Some individuals come closer than others, but it is not made easy for them by their own religions. There is one more thing I would like to say here and that is the act of killing your brother or sister in the name of God is a lie, all such deaths have nothing to do with God.

9

SOON IT WILL BE time to choose your own path, and which way will you turn and walk? You can chose to walk following someone who is enticing you down a path of darkness, saying it doesn't matter how much pain you cause yourself or someone else. Crucially, this is the one thing that does matter. When you provide pain as a food you are feeding those you would run screaming from if you could see them, were you not blind to the higher dimensions. Not all of you are blind; trust yourselves and others who have extra sight. There's a complete world out there.

I have another path that consists of light. Steps taken along this path allow you to experience joy. Some of you have never experienced true joy welling up and spilling out of your hearts. It is the other side of darkness: joy. Joy is light, and living in the light, and is yours if you want to walk that way and create it for yourself. *Does this give me joy and make me joyful?* There is no truer compass for any of you. I want you to focus on joy and seek it out, seek out what gives you joy beyond measure and be in the space of light, and share your joy with everyone. Most of you have no idea what this could be like, and I know it could be frightening to some, to be so happy. You're not used to it much living on Earth. When something happens for the first time it can be hard, but it gets easier as it's repeated. This goes for joy as well as acts of violence and darkness. Practice walking in the light, practice being joyful.

10

OVER TIME THIS PLANET has had to subsist on energy as unlike its own as can be. This planet Earth was not by nature a planet without joy. Like all other planets it is a planet that has joy and light as part of its makeup. The effect of being alive while there is darkness and hatred like a layer of mud on her surface has had the effect of smothering her, and poisoning her. Wherever this is removed by those who will not tolerate it by protecting their own area, they give themselves a wholesome and healthy place to live and provide a breathing space for the planet. In the absence of serious Earth healing by society as a whole, it is society as community that holds the darkness at bay. You can see this where society has broken down and there is a lot of killing. These areas hold the energy of hatred and violence beyond the time of the killing event. There is much to be cleared from many, many areas of the planet even after the killing stops.

The way to clear away what has been left behind is for the Earth to be honoured and served. Stop poisoning it, and start healing it. Resume the Reiki circles described by Melchizadek. Allow the love that brings you to spend your time healing in circles to extend beyond and care for the physical planet. When she is brought back to health you will see her as she can be; a paradise home for your soul group.

The previous soul groups who have lived here all honoured this planet. They were grateful for her generosity, and her willingness to be of service. Why else would she tolerate some of the games she has hosted, all risky to herself? She should be acknowledged for what she is, your loving home planet. There has never been another for the human race.

When decisions are taken to abuse her, where are the rest of you, why are you not protecting her? There are whole mountain ranges being levelled in your names so you can use the coal contained in them. That is only one small example of the poisoning and destruction happening on her surface. If you saw anyone being treated the way you are treating this planet you would have a legal case and punish the ones doing the damage. "We didn't know she was alive." But I think that as you looked at what was happening you knew it was wrong, didn't you?

11

WHEN HUMANITY FIRST incarnated here as a splintered soul group, it was able to do many things that you would find hard to believe now. There was an ease of communication through telepathy, and an ease of death and dying as people voluntarily laid down their lives before they became infirm. They walked with a light step on the Earth. Remember all those flying dreams you've had in your childhood? Part of you remembers not being Earthbound. The seas were a second home, how many of you delight in time submerged in a swimming pool or a bath? You were here, but not so fixed or limited, not so sure that you wanted to just walk on the dry land. That came later. In the beginning your soul group tried out different variations.

As time went by you chose dry land and living together in communities. Why am I mentioning this now? Some of your lost abilities are about to resurface and be reused. You may find you can use telepathy beyond having a 'feeling' that someone wants to speak to you, or thinking of a person one day and having them call you the next. These 'coincidences' are using your natural inborn abilities, and you have many more of them. Telepathy is popular and understandable to talk about, but there are more that are going to take you by surprise. When something unexpected happens to you, remember this and enjoy reaching further into an understanding of what is happening, and learn to use it again. There is so much more to being human than you have been used to using. Do not at any time fear the new and unusual, but give everyone the space to develop and use their talents.

Sometimes you may find there is a person showing great talent who is restrained and locked up. Remember that it is yourself being locked away, that you also have that very same ability or talent. When this happens do not be afraid of this person who flies past your window, but consider how you may do it yourself. Question all those who would deny you your birthright.

When the days come where you begin finding out the truth about who you are as a species; remember that we will be there with you, helping you to find out. As has been said before, the truth is a form of light. Where there is light and truth, lies have a harder time to exist. Every time someone says you cannot be telepathic it is to keep you from trying and believing that you are more than you are. You are all much more than you are; you are tiny particles of God and everyone knows he is able to hear thoughts directed at him. Remember who you are.

A long time ago when you were new on this planet you spoke to the stars and heard their replies; walked among the trees and conversed with them and the many life forms that sheltered there. All of this is still possible for you. It will only happen when you realise that all things on this planet have their own souls and their own lives and purposes. Many, many life forms have contracted to be here and learn their own lessons about God. How can you say that your lesson is superior to theirs? Or that their purpose here is to serve you? Your blindness has made you lethal to the others living here at the same time as you. Whole species have been wiped out, gone; as if it didn't matter that their game was terminated early by humans. It mattered to them. They are waiting to come back and finish their games, but some of them are waiting for you to leave first. Others will return before then as they have a commitment to the planet that they will come back and keep. These will not always be in the same form. The life forms that return are to be honoured for their commitment to their game and the planet.

12

OPEN YOUR EYES; really open them when you are looking around you. Practice looking beyond the three dimensional physical world by considering what the energy of the object is that you are looking at. Look for an additional shape or shimmer, something out of the corner of your eye perhaps. There is no reason for you not to be able to see further into higher dimensions than you were able to previously. This takes you back a few hundred years to the time before you were told you were bad or wrong to see higher dimensions, before you were burned as witches by the ruling church. There is much in the fifth dimension that you can see right now, and by that I mean the elementals. Look for the shimmer of their passing and don't be afraid. They are concerned with the planet, not with you, they are our co-workers and we share many of the same goals. They act out of love. The next time someone says they've seen a fairy see if you can see it yourself. The easiest thing in the world is for those who are blind and can't see to laugh at those who can. Why is this? Why do you listen to the blind among you at all? Find friends who do not laugh and learn how to be more than you are now. Laughter and making fun of those who can see is a power game. If they can stop you they can control you. At this time we would wish to see some support for those with deeper sight, turn away from those who laugh and listen to what some people are seeing in the world around them. Learn to navigate your way safely through the crowds of higher dimensional beings that join you on this planet. I urge you to practice this for your own safety and advancement towards the light. One day those who are blind will be ashamed to admit they have no sight and ask for help in seeing, but that will not happen just yet.

Now that I have asked you to open your eyes and look around you some of you will do just that, and you will see more than elementals. There are legions of dark angels here on this planet, and you need to learn how to live and not give them your energy. You need to be able to say "I will have nothing to do with you, be gone into the light." That is a very powerful thing to say to a demon, for you control your own space.

So many of you who have had mental problems, and physical problems have been playing host to these demons. What if when you went to a doctor he could just remove them and send you on your way? For some people this would be enough. You have no idea how it looks from here. Demons are attracted to the weak and the strong, the old and the young. Anytime you are concerned about what is going on around you ask for our help and ask that they are removed and transformed into light, all of them around you and in your homes. Do not put up with them and give them your life. I know this part is uncomfortable to read, but you are not alone with them anymore, and they can't stay when you demand that they go.

The dark angels have been here as long as you have on this planet, and you have made it so easy for them by blinding yourselves to the higher dimensions. They need you to give them your energy to thrive and grow in strength, and this is what they latch onto and take. They don't ask your permission first, they just entwine themselves around you and draw away your energy. They also can influence and control people. This happens at different levels, from very slightly to a controlled puppet. Sometimes there is behaviour that is inexplicable to you, a level of wrongdoing that seems to come out of nowhere. It doesn't really come from nowhere; it is just an example of how these dark angels are able to live here and turn a loving planet into a place that is fighting for her life.

They do not have the right to do this, they are using humans, but they can be stopped. They can be stopped because you are a tiny replica of God, and you are each individually powerful enough to tell them to leave your space and be taken into the light. At that point they will go as you are in control of your body and space, not them. This is hardly ever done as very few realise that they have this problem, and your scientists and doctors consider this realisation as a symptom of insanity. For this reason it is best to clear yourself from time to time of *anything and everything that has no right to be in your body and aura, and have it transformed into light.* Make it harder for them to hold onto this planet.

This infiltration of the human population began here so long ago, it is nothing new. It is not how you really are, a soul of deadly killing and destruction. You are a soul with inherent good, like so many other souls in this universe. Your incessant wars, from gang wars on your city streets, to tribal genocides in Africa are not who you are. We of the light remember you from your beginning here, and you are light, the makeup of your soul is light. You can each individually be that again now, and if the number of people on this planet shed the dark layers that have attached to them, and have them transformed into light (important!) there will be an increase in light itself here. If you simply have something removed and walk away, what is to stop it from latching on to the next person it sees? Help yourselves and this planet by transforming them into light yourself.

13

HERE WE ARE THEN, at a time when everything is preparing to change, and when great things that were long planned are set to happen. Help is coming for this planet in the near future. What will your role be when that time comes? Will you be ready to step forward and work with the cosmic forces arriving here in a few years? Will you be exactly the same as you are now, having discussions on where you can next strip mine coal, dump toxic waste, or run an oil pipeline? There will be a lot of help here for Earth, and what would it be like if the human population were once again actively healing her? If you like to think about your soul ascending, which way do you think leads along that route? It's still possible that you may not ascend, that you will counteract much that is being done for this planet and all the plans and effort will not be enough. I wouldn't count on someone else's efforts to carry you along; I would recommend that each of you do your very best to help the Earth. As angelic beings we can see the benefits of the healing circles, but we do not disregard the actual physical work put in by humans. It is work given in love and it is also necessary and effective. Some of you are acting the way *all of you* will need to, in order for this to work in a sustainable way.

The time that you are all looking forward to with anticipation is the year 2012, when there will be extraordinary changes in the energy coming to this planet. The intention is that the planet Earth will be able to receive this energy directly, be bathed in it as it were. It will be powerful and specific in its intention and goals. It will be for her, not for you. She is ready to receive it now, except for one thing: there aren't many places that it can reach her through the layer of thick darkness you humans have surrounded her with. Your job over the next few years is to change yourself and your energy you have put around her. Change fear into joy, and start laughter in motion again. The economic changes that are in place now are good changes, changes for the better. Do not fear them, and do not fear for yourselves at this time. We look at all of this from our vantage point and say, finally now things are going to shift and a light shine into some very dark corners. You are at the beginning of a time of great change, every bit of which is necessary for you. The better you are able to let go of your attachment to the old ways and the status quo, the easier you will find your journey through this time.

This is the end time for certain useless ideas and beliefs that will not stand up in the light of day. This will come as a shock to many of you who have lived your lives being deceived by those who implied you could trust them completely with your well-being. When the light of truth shines onto those who have held power for long ages and their maggoty faces are seen for what they are they will be finished. At this point most of them cannot imagine this happening; they can't conceive of a time that will be any different from the past where they lived off the subjugation of others by force or by deception. The rest of you can look forward to being free of those who have despoiled you and the planet to keep their hands on wealth and power. There will finally be greater freedom and equality for all, and a better life for all of you.

By working to allow the energy to blanket the Earth and reach her through the human crust you will all be working with the cosmic energies of love, light and truth. Helping her will help you. Walking on a planet in full health that is getting what she needs will affect you through your feet and the very air you breathe. When her own light shines more strongly you will walk in the light more easily and take strength from her health. She is eager and ready to make any change that will restore her to herself. She's been a prisoner for a long, long time of the darkness that lives here.

I am coming to the end of my chapter now and I have only these few final words. The light is coming back to this planet but it can still be blocked and kept out. Therefore everything that you can do in a personal way for yourself and for the planet that will increase the light here is necessary to tip the balance from dark to light. You will have all the help the angels of light in this universe can give you, but it is up to you as the soul in residence on this planet to reject the darkness in yourself. Walk away from fear and those who preach violence, excuse yourself from their presence and activities. Take positive, personal action on how you live and what manner of items you buy for yourself. Recycle and buy only what you truly need and do not support those industries that destroy the planet you live on. This is so obvious, so mundane, and you've heard it all before. Pay attention and change yourself; this is vitally important. Living in a sustainable way is the only way to live, and any other way is a web of dark lies. The other way is how you got into this mess.

Section Three

A View from
the Dark Side

ARCHANGEL OF DARKNESS

1

I AM MELCHIOR, THE ANGEL of Dark. I am the angel who opposes the Angel of Light in all parts of this universe. I have been given a place to write in this book by Melchizadek so that you may understand that even the dark is an aspect of God. I wish to illuminate the dark places of the universe for you so that you can comprehend the magnitude and characteristics of the dark.

At all times I strive against the light so that worlds will come under my influence. This involves banishing the light and all that it stands for, for although I came from the light myself, it is not my role to tolerate it. When a planet is mine and given over to me; the lessons learned there also teach the Creator about himself. These lessons are as much a part of the whole as all the lessons of light. My lessons involve suffering and misery it is true, and subterfuge and lies, but that is how you will know me and all my works. Look to the hidden acts, the secret words and you will find me. I am everywhere.

This opportunity to speak to you directly is being closely monitored by Melchizadek and the other angels of light. If I attempt to weave a web of deception I will not be allowed to contribute, and they are aware of the truth as much as I am. Just because I work with lies doesn't mean I don't know what is and isn't true. Melchizadek also holds the channel in his protection and I am only allowed to speak to her through him. That means that any lies I try to tell will be picked up by him first and removed. We have known each other since the beginning and he knows me and my ways well.

In the beginning we started in a universe that was evenly balanced between light and dark. I soon saw that the easiest way to tip the balance in my favour was to deal in lies. Lies keep the correct information hidden so that when choices are made they are made on a false basis. Like a tower built on a crooked, rotten base lie after lie builds up to a crooked twisted building. At this point the population usually doesn't know how to start untangling the mess that has been made. It is so effective to work through lies that I prefer it to murder or war; although those are the result, not the cause of lies. Your recent wars have all been based on lies; all fought for reasons other than the ones stated when the young men and women were being shipped to foreign shores. Some wars of neighbour against neighbour are based on the lie of scarcity; that there is not enough of something to go around. It doesn't have to be any more sophisticated than that. Recent wars have all been fought over power, the power to control resources. I don't think the ones dying were the ones to benefit from the control over resources.

The fact that you value these goods and resources at all is based on falseness. You have no need of many of the things you are fighting over. But I convinced you that you did need these things, and it was worth killing to have them. You may be thinking, "not me, I never killed anyone;" but it was done in your name by those who were willing. You didn't kill anyone and take gasoline or petrol for your cars, but you allowed many wars to be fought over it so you could keep on the move. Think of all those who died in Stalingrad for oil, and all those who die now in the Middle East. What would make you let this be done in your name? Lies.

I know you humans, blind as newborn mice and as ineffective, although you see yourselves as knowledgeable and moral. You are so ignorant of all that exists around you. You walk on a planet of twelve dimensions, of which you only see three, and you thought you could come here to this planet and play this game and there would be some point to it. The point to it all was that you fell for one of my more ingenious lies before you ever set this up. The prize is here, this planet is what we were playing for and you came in to play a game blindfolded with your hands tied behind your backs. It was so easy to pick you off from the beginning. Your game was designed with that fatal flaw with my guidance, of course. You thought that if you could find out more about being God from the most disadvantageous start in the universe that everyone would think you were the greatest soul who had played the most extreme game. You like extreme sports on your planet, and this is the mind-set of a being that elected to play this ridiculous game. I was able to sweep in with the darkness almost from the very beginning.

This one does not like to channel me. But I have many who listen to my whispers and pass on my lies. What is the reason for allowing me space in this book? My role in this universe is to promote the dark, to seize control of the entire universe and people it with my own dark entities and energy, so that when the game ends this universe is mine. I will not easily give up anything to the light.

I am the dark, created by the One who created us all in his perfection and his wisdom. My purpose in this universe, in any universe is to give contrast to the light. When all is bright white or deepest blackness there is no way to distinguish the shape or pattern of anything. The game of black on black is dull, there is nothing to look at, no lessons to be drawn from it. How do you expect to learn about what it is to be God if there is no way to tell what it is you are learning? The white stroke on the black background is certainly hard to miss. You can't see the light without the dark to give it shape. That is why the games where the most to be learned are those on the planets where both are present, and where it is balanced on a knife edge. Your planet is not balanced yet. Your planet is still mine at the present. I maintain my hold on the majority of the populations, and in particular the institutions with power. It will be a while before the balance is ever reached.

This book would seem to be the last thing I would want to see published. I have been busy fighting it on the other dimensions to prevent its being written at all. I have my own motives for participating; I have desired to speak directly to you myself for long ages. I am not an angel of light, or a fallen angel, or anything that you may have associated with me. I am not a devil with horns and cloven feet. I am an angel of God, created to champion the dark and its entire works. All That Is includes the dark as well as the light. You could say half of creation, currently under my care, is dark. And what do you humans say about it, and do about it? You shun it as coming from somewhere other than God. It is not possible to have anything that does not come from God. It has a purpose, and there are many new lessons that can be learned by turning to face it and seeing what it is all about.

2

NOW SOME OF you may be quivering and thinking I don't want to get any closer, thank you, or see what is there. May I suggest you start with the night sky and see how my dark sets off the brilliance of the stars? How the shadow gives definition and shape to the painting or photograph, a 3-D representation of two dimensions? How the courage of the hero in battle shines against the killing surrounding him? Dark lets the light shine brighter and all is for the glory of the Creator. Learn about the reasons for the dark by observing it. One day when you are faced with your own darkness you will recognise it as providing the opportunity for your own light to shine at its brightest. And everyone; everyone has a dark side. Those of you who live whole lives will know you are not all light, for your Creator created us out of himself. The dark is holy too.

When someone explores and acknowledges their inner demons, their inner darkness they go through a process of shining light on them, and bringing them forward into the light. How do I feel about that? Shouldn't I wish everyone to sink into blackness? Keep their inner demons and pain festering away and making them miserable? The game is the Creator learning about himself and my role is within that game. Learning about yourself is part of your own role as a Creator. I facilitate all of you Creators learning about yourselves. And in that way the Creator of us all learns about himself. I am a faithful servant of the Dark, and I provide the dark so that the light can be seen.

You little blind humans have so much trouble seeing anything at all that my game and lessons on this planet have been extremely successful for a very long time. You would not have noticed any subtle games, and I have used a large canvas and painted it liberally with wars, genocide and man-made famines. I take my work seriously, as seriously as the light take theirs. I have a job to do, and I devote myself to doing it. I instigate war and disaster, and I use humans to carry out whatever is necessary to make sure they happen. You can always tell who my faithful servants are.

Today I observe this planet from my position as overlord and I am satisfied. I have caused you to decimate whole continents with your destructive ways. If you cannot kill one another with weapons, you leave behind famine in your wake so the enemy will die of hunger. Little of real help is given to those who are dying like this. You are all very far from seeing yourself in your neighbours' eyes. So your original goal of finding God from a place of complete unknowing looks like coming true as you work your way through levels of hell to find him with my help. At this point in time I am winning here so comprehensively that I have nothing to complain about.

3

THE SITUATION ON Earth is changing so swiftly now that your planet is becoming unrecognisable to me. Perhaps you think I should mind if this planet swings back to the light. I do mind, and will do everything in my power to keep this planet under my control. I am the dark and it is my role to keep this planet, and all other dark planets as part of my empire. What you can expect to see in the coming years is my forces fighting harder than ever to keep this planet for me. I can do nothing else but try to hang onto this prize planet. I want this planet as mine.

Why not just let me stay here and learn the most you can from being a planet in balance? I'm afraid that this planet has had enough of me and my kind and is ready to move on now into the light herself. She is ready to play at a higher dimensional level and start afresh as an ascended planet of light. The one thing that can stop her reaching her ascended level at this time is you, so you are the ones I will be working with to prevent that. You are so easy to work with. Although other planets have played variations on these games, only you chose the blindfold. And you never dreamed in the beginning that you would splinter so many times, six billion splinters now who have no idea they are all one. So many of you are ready to kill each other over *nothing*; over trivial loot like a cell phone. It is a wonderful planet for me to be on. Long may it continue; and I don't accept balance, I am always striving for the dark.

The dark needs representation here and on all planets. On those planets that have suffered and learned from the dark, and have chosen to move on into the light or ascended when they had the opportunity I am no longer present. They are planets of light now. They finished their growth through the dark phase and are balanced in the light and contribute to the light. I have my own planets that completely lost touch with the light and are enclosed in darkness. They are balanced in the darkness. There is almost no opportunity for them to move into the light, until now. If this planet is able to shake off the darkness, that is sunk so very deep, then anything can happen. There are many who are watching what is happening here. I don't think you can do it, and I'm not about to write anything to encourage you to try to get rid of me. This is my happy home, full of my friends and relations.

4

NOW FOR THE inside information: how bad is it? Why am I so confident that speaking the truth for once in a book will not set me back on this planet? Why have I agreed to write here at all? This planet has been colonised and eaten away by my most faithful dark angels. There are nests burrowed into the Earth and monstrous beings of darkness surrounding you at all times feeding off your misery, weakening you and changing you into my creatures. You as a soul are no longer showing light, you show unhappiness and cruelty. Those who are light are so few and far between that I do not regard them as threats to my rule. Did Nelson Mandela or Ghandi turn their countries into sweetness and light? I could not work with them so I worked with those surrounding them. In other countries the leaders (secular and religious) were mine and they had the easy job of dragging their people straight into the dark behind them. You will know who I mean if you are paying any attention while reading this book.

Once a world is this far gone into my darkness I feel that my victory is assured. You no longer remember what it is like to be open and happy, and what it is to love. You have no love for yourself or for anyone else, you actually shy away from those who openly love; it's a bit too much isn't it? Those people are a bit weird, aren't they? Talking about love, showing love to all no matter who they are. You don't know what to say to them if they meet you on the street. I have managed to turn open love into one of my weapons of darkness. Now that love is suspicious, how and what are you going to do to reintroduce love as light? I'm quite pleased about that one.

Fear of love, fear of your fellow human, fear as the top priority of governments and citizens. What does all this fear make you do, how does it make you feel? Like loving strangers unconditionally? I don't think so; that is why I rank fear right up there with lies as my favourite tools. Fear keeps you separated, isolated, and *lonely*. I like lonely, show me a lonely person who is happy. Show me a country full of separated and isolated people that is strong. The seeds of your own destruction are bound up in your levels of fear.

5

Y OU HAVE TO GO back to the idea that the human soul was somehow going to get through this game as a blind baby without hurting anyone. Is it possible that there was an initial disregard for this planet in the design of your game that is still so obvious today? Look at the condition of this planet. Look at your actions towards her on a daily basis, hourly basis. This planet is a despised trash world to you. I would like to claim credit for all of this, but I think you need to acknowledge some responsibility. For once I am not trying to induce guilt; I'm just stating the obvious. Arrogance is not an attribute of the light.

For a long time now you humans have taken, taken, taken from this planet. Even when there were very few of you here you began to alter the bounteous landscape you were provided with to live in. You were the ones who designed a planet that had everything you needed for life, and for your game here. As soon as you could grow grass from the seed heads to make bread, or ancient wheat, you altered what was here. Your planet adapted and continued to provide food and shelter for you but after a while many of your agricultural practices created accelerated erosion, or poisoning as in the case of almost all bodies of water now. I don't mind, I have other sources of nourishment. But what are you thinking, you humans, to poison your water and turn your planet into a desert? I may be the darkness between the stars, but I am still part of the Creator. The love of the Creator that permeates through every part of his creation still exists inside me. I see a race of beings here that is so far removed from that love that their behaviour is incomprehensible even to me. That doesn't mean I'm objecting to this behaviour, indeed I am the only one prepared to take advantage of it. At least someone is benefiting, even if you're not.

Why am I saying all these helpful things to you, shredding the illusion that there is no God, no light, no dark, no good, or bad? Why contribute to a book that could reduce my position or help the light at all? Can you believe or trust a word written here by me? I am the Angel of Darkness, created out of love by the Creator of all. I fulfil my role with integrity, knowing my contributions to God learning about himself are perhaps the most valuable of all. Whatever you think about my actions or the results that stem from them, know this – I am as beloved as any Angel of Light ever is. My role is harder in many ways; for I bring to God the lessons learned by misery and pain, and these are very far from love. No matter how far into darkness a soul group or a planet travels, when the end is reached there is only God. Travel to God by blissfully ascending into the light if you can, but if you cannot I will escort you there anyway by my joyless paths. When all games end there is only the return to the Creator. All there is will return to All There Is. There is nowhere else to go.

I am Melchior, an Archangel you would call me if you ever heard my name. And I belong in the ranks of the highest with Melchizadek and my brother Lucifer, the Angel of Light. Too long has he been penalised by those who knew better, and knew who he really was. But it was such a good trick to convince you that light was dark, and dark was light. Who would listen to Lucifer and learn about the light if they were too frightened of him to deal with him? This ranks up with the 'God is Dead' lie for usefulness and amusement. Just because I am beloved by the Creator don't forget who I really am and what my role is. I take pride in the quality of my work, and let's face it; I'm ahead in the game on this planet Earth.

Section Four

Techniques to Bring Yourself Closer to the Light

ARCHANGEL ARIEL

1

I AM THE ARCHANGEL ARIEL, and I sometimes act as a technician. I'm very good at working out what needs to be done and how to do it. You humans are at a point where if you begin to do some things differently you will start to make a difference. After all, you can't keep on doing the same things in the same ways and expect everything to suddenly improve!

I have some suggestions to make to the population of the planet as a whole, and some suggestions that are focused on those who have been following a path of light for some time – some more advanced techniques shall we say?

When you look at the other humans on your planet you are very good at seeing the differences between you that make you each unique. Most of you are not good at seeing that you are really all the same; that the differences are so minute that to other eyes they barely exist. We are not looking at your physical selves because we can see the person inside, and on the inside you are one and the same. Disregard the outside envelope and see the soul within. When you look at another species or animal are you struck by their similarities or differences? The focus on differences between one person and another, particularly in regards to *gender,* more so than skin colour has based your lives on a false foundation. True sight shows you all to be one soul in many bodies.

2

I N THE BEGINNING you knew everything I am going to tell you. You were living in a gracious land and had a deep love for, and gratitude to, the planet that was giving you such a beautiful home, and you never chose to act abusively. Now I am going to have to instruct you on how to live with a planet and not abuse her or harm her, but live *with* her. It's a little sad, even to an angel. But I am glad of the opportunity to talk to a new audience. Some of you will be thinking this isn't new or magical; it's just the same things the environmentalists have been preaching at us for years. Who do you think many of those environ-mentalists are? Angels are incarnate here in force during these important days.

You have many opportunities to change your ways, and altering your lifestyle behaviour is one I hope you already know. Walk and bicycle instead of driving, downsize your homes and equipment so you use less fuel and pollute less heavily, all of these are more important than you know. There are some of you that are using the Earth so heavily, so destructively in your consumption of oil and other fuels that you cannot be thinking at all of the future that is just around the corner. Look honestly at your carbon footprint and reduce it to zero, and stop being a burden and part of the problem. What happens if you don't? What happens to the Earth when she runs out of the carbon fuels you are merrily burning? She will not be the same.

The Earth has stores of carbon to balance gases on her surface; it allows her to adjust the atmosphere as required by different species. You think because your life spans are so very short that she makes no adjustments herself. She is a self-regulating being and sensitive to the needs of all who live on her. Remember you are not the first species to have lived here. Your needs were catered for once upon a time until you, yourselves altered your own atmosphere by digging up carbon stores and burning them. They will be gone one day and you will have changed the air you breathe into something foul. Then what are you going to do for air?

Here is what I would like to see you do: use the technology you already have to insulate and cut down on all fuel use now while you prepare to switch over to clean energies. The acceptable energy productions for these days are solar, wind, geothermal and tidal. Combined with *using less* of everything this will give the planet, and you, a short breathing space. The important thing here is the message that you are changing, and are ready to change completely towards harmless energy sources. Why is this so important? Because the Earth can provide all of your energy needs cleanly, herself. She just isn't going to do that for you right now. Not until you stop harming her first.

A long time ago, when the Atlanteans were provided with Earth energy through the generator crystals they had all the energy that they could use. They used it for heat and light as well as scientific experiments. They powered the machine that split souls into male/female with crystal energy, and a huge quantity was required for that. As their experiments progressed they took for granted that the energy was there for them to use, and they became greedy in their energy consumption. As was described earlier many of the experiments they performed were inspired by the dark angels with hideous results. The Earth was deeply unhappy about her gift being used to increase the amount of pain on her surface. She was drawn into participation with the experiments by providing the energy, and it was abhorrent to her.

The Earth was an unwilling partner to those experiments, and more was more happening than cloning at that time. There was the grafting of body parts together from various species to see what kind of new animal they could make; as if the original animals had no consciousness to be abused! Would the animal live afterwards, or die? There was some human/animal grafting also, of all kinds and descriptions. The stylised illustrations from ancient Egypt of their Gods were a far cry from the reality of these experiments. There was so much callousness towards the ones used in this, dismembered and put together "just to see", and if they would make a new sort of useful slave. One slave they created stood tall, at almost two metres, with a body similar to a wolf spider but with the huge powerful shoulders of a man. There were eight powerful arms each ending in a human hand. This creature lived in the heat at the bottom of a mine where his power and dexterity allowed him to be the machine that handled the ropes and levers like a living machine. Surrounded by humans he bellowed his confusion and pain, he had no idea why he was made like this or treated this way. When people create a child they treat it with love and respect, but these poor creatures were never given love and respect by their creators. These people should never have created these forms of life. We could see by this more than in any other way that Atlanteans had lost their ability to live and act with love and respect. Rest in peace all those created during those last days.

There was a total disregard for all life as an aspect of the Creator. Without the energy provided by crystals they would not have been able to weld them together with light. My memories of those days fill me with sadness.

The crystal energy was removed prior to the end of Atlantis by agreement between the Earth and the crystals, to protect the crystals. After that time, for the time remaining until the removal of the continent, they burned wood fires, some coal, and some whale oil. Plunged into primitive semi-darkness what do you think they did? There were human sacrifices as village attacked neighbouring village, tricked into thinking that these sacrifices would make the Earth bring back her crystal energy. They were considering drilling into the Earth for oil just before we lifted the continent out. In fact, that was the final straw as we did not want the continent punctured, or the oil drawn out, or the energy provided for any more malicious experiments. Following Atlantis there was never enough energy available until the Industrial Revolution for wide-scale experiments, and that was a good thing.

We do not look too kindly on your global oil industry. Fuel comes from somewhere and I refer you to photographs of the sacred lands of the Athabasca River in Alberta, Canada among others. Think about what has to take place to provide you with your gasoline and petrol. At the time of writing I know that you are not ready to give up your cars, but I want you to think carefully about your journeys and to always look for alternatives to travelling by fuel.

3

WE LOOK AT the way you live today, and what is the Earth's life blood being used for? You run a large machine two minutes down the road to pick up some milk while your bodies ache for exercise. It may take the complete and total absence of petrol and gasoline to finally get you out of your cars. You've heard it all before and never paid any attention. But these are the things that can make a difference today, leaving your car behind and walking or bicycling on those short journeys. Dust off your bikes and get pedalling! Do everything in your power to reduce the fuel you use.

I am here to point out these physical solutions because they are important. They go hand in hand with loving the Earth, and caring for her wellbeing. Many of you have heard and disregarded these messages in the past, but to change your *own* habits is all that you can do. You can't change anyone else's. These actions would be taken out of loving care for her, and acting from love is an action of light. Your light will shine out a little brighter and show others a new way of living. You will be able to look around in your own pool of light and see a little farther and with greater understanding. One day there will be enough light shining from enough individuals joining together, so that the darkness will be gone in some areas, and the light will spread. When the light spreads you will really be able to *see,* part of the reason you are not all able to see the reality around you is the sheer amount of darkness lying on this planet.

What we see when we look at the Earth is very different from what you see. You look at green grass and plants growing but we see death, a planet dying by slow suffocation. Her surface is black and all but a few trees are gone, and they are dying. Which is the reality, and why are we seeing differently? You are veiled to all but the first three dimensions and they will be the last to show this destruction. But they will show it one day if it isn't reversed. When you want to create something good for yourself in your life it always starts in the higher dimensions and works its way downwards to you energetically into the solidity of your world. What we see is the energetic reality that has been created here, that is trickling down to the reality of your world. As the energetic picture of this world has changed; so will the physical surface. It looks deader than the aftermath of an Australian bush fire, because there you would expect new shoots to grow in the rain. This dying energy is what we are going to ask you to work to reverse, by rejecting it and working to create the energy of a living and healthy planet.

The last lifestyle habit I want to mention before moving on is the production of energy by the filthy and harmful method of nuclear power stations. What are you thinking, to produce energy in a way that leaves toxic poison lying around the planet afterwards? It doesn't matter to the planet whether it is buried under her skin or dumped in her oceans, it's still stuck to her and it burns. You have no idea of the harm you are doing with this form of generating energy. The uses you have for energy go so far beyond the basics of comfort and light, and your produce so much energy just so you can waste it on not turning off your electrical equipment when it is not being used. Please stop being such a burden to the Earth.

Now that I've mentioned the obvious concerning your physical reality I would like to go back to the energetic steps that you can take as individuals and as groups.

4

A LONG TIME AGO there was a split between the desirable world and your world. It happens sometimes, that a timeline and projection that everyone thinks is going to go forward, fails. In this case the main projection, the broadest and strongest timeline carried forward into the future of the Earth and her human population was rural. You can visit this agrarian world in books and literature now, in well-known books such as J.R.R. Tolkien's Lord of the Rings and C.S. Lewis's Chronicles of Narnia books. These books in particular show the world that was to have been your world. Narnia, the land of health and beauty with room for everyone to share in partnership together, is your lost world. You lost some of it before the industrial revolution when people stopped seeing the elementals, and the rest went with the new machines. There are quite a few angel-inspired fantasy sagas out there today. Some of your fiction writers can see along this other, original timeline and place their stories there.

Take a moment to remember the pre-industrial revolution where clean air and water were taken for granted. Clean air and water are requirements for human, animal, plant and planetary life.

When you look at the timelines streaming out from any given moment in time on this planet you can see them fan out and branch over and over again, so that there can be many choices how the future will unfold. Even so there are broader, straighter roads which are cultivated by us; and those by the dark angels also. Sometimes we have quite a hard time wrenching the timelines back to the light. So in addition to everything else, the dark and the light are fighting over the future, and how events will unfold. At the time of the industrial revolution we lost control of the future to the dark angels. At first the new inventions seemed like they were so much better and moving around on trains in the UK was an improvement even if the air was made black with the burning coal. But goods had always gone to market before there were trains. In fact people had always managed to do and have *enough* before then. You have so much now that you look back to the past and think it was hard work and it was boring. You work so much harder now than in the past, and work lonelier. The truth is that people were connected together more then than they are now; they were closer to knowing themselves and their Creator then because they were still in contact with the Earth.

Do you remember how the darkness began to be a problem first in the cities of Atlantis? It was because they had less contact with the planet itself. You are here in partnership with the Earth, she can help you find yourself, and finding yourself is all you came here to do. Her role is to provide her surface for the game and out of love, and assist you to finish in a blaze of light.

When the population moved into the cities, a process that is still happening across the globe, many people were removed from regular contact with the Earth. There is an ever increasing proportion of the Earth's population living in cities now, and it grows larger every day. People are weaker without contact with the Earth to help them resist the darkness that thrives there and creates darkness in the soul. She would help you if she could.

The city populations today suffer more than any previous group in your history. Think about the vast cities of China, or Lagos in Nigeria. Lives are lived there in dirty air and water, with never enough of anything and still they work so hard to live their lives and provide for their children. They don't know how to go back to the countryside they came from, to find a place to live there and start over. The farming skills of previous generations have not always been passed on. They thought that moving into a city would bring more. More what? The knowledge of what one needs to live well and healthily with contentment in modern life is gone. The connection to the Earth is broken. She goes her way and you go yours.

How do you change this big picture? Remember, I mentioned that you still had a few centuries to go before you would be ready to join together. What can you do personally to change any of this, or turn the clock back in a sensible way? You can only take the body and life that you have and live differently.

5

THERE ARE MANY things you can do to alter the picture we see of the Earth as a planet on its last legs. First, stop harming it through carelessness or maliciousness. This is IMPORTANT! Second, and at the same time, treat her with love and care for her. How do you treat someone you love, a partner or a child? You give them what they need to be healthy and happy, and protect them from harm. What does the Earth need from all of you?

Take for example, her surface, her energetic skin. It's like the surface tension on a drop of water, so fragile and easily destroyed. This skin contains the energetic self of the Earth; she exists inside the planet filling it as you fill your own body. You see solid ground, we see transparent energy. We see more, that the nature of this energetic planet is fluid and lively; she needs to be able to dance with joy. So wobbling is a good thing for her, and being able to adjust is a sign of health. After all, she has been frozen in dirt for a long time now and she's feeling a need to stretch. But she remembers her agreed role as your home and sticks to her agreement. This role will not last forever for her as long as you are ready to move on and ascend together as one soul.

Freeing the Earth involves you coming together as one soul, acknowledging your kinship with all other humans on this planet. And now we come back to the hard part for many, many of you. You are taught that you are different, and of course, better than others. Culturally every skin tone looks at another and thinks, I'm so glad my skin isn't that colour, and that I was born with the best colour. You don't see the beauty present in all people, denying kinship. You don't look in another's eyes and see yourself looking back. Not yet, but you will. And that is the hope and promise of these days; the days that will see you humans turn everything around once and for all.

So first, unite! You, as an individual reading this book, look at the next one hundred and fifty people you see right in the eye and think inside this wonderful person is me and I may find wholeness by finally acknowledging this. I see the eyes of God looking back at me. I will practice this exercise until I *know* that we are all one and the same, we are splinters of the same soul.

This deliberate searching for yourself in the eyes of another is an extension of the search for your soul mate, so popular in today's world. When you begin to see how big you are, how big a soul you have and how it is present in so many beautiful people there will be a real change. You will begin to value all human life. Remember that you can only change yourself. This may seem like a small piece of effort to be made to reunite all the warring factions of the world. So small that you can't believe that this is the bit of magic that will change everything. This is the first step; to look with love and recognition at all you meet.

Think about how it is right now in your life, how you meet strangers during the day with shutters over your eyes. You are oblivious that all you encounter are the same as you. You do not connect with them soul to soul. You rarely make eye contact with strangers. What happens when you engage with the person at the till when out shopping? When you are fully open and available to them in love? Try it.

The act of going from no recognition to love will shock your soul with an electric shock of joy. There is the joy of connection, an end to loneliness for one second, and progress in the game. You all actually know about the game you are contracted here to play, deep down in your subconscious minds. You chose to look for God wearing blindfolds, and just as someone who is playing Blind Man's Bluff, you know you are in a game. If you had played Blind Man's Bluff for say, thirty-eight years with no progress, and you suddenly laid your hands on someone else and connected, what would you feel? Joy and relief that you had actually somehow finally done it. So this is what is waiting for you as an individual; finding yourself in another's eyes. If everyone who reads this book finds themselves in the eyes of all they meet they will stop being the separate splinter, and the human soul will walk on the pathway of love. It is hard to fight wars with those you love, hate will be less prevalent and the energy will be set for the second step.

6

SECONDLY, WHEN YOU HAVE cracked open the separate shell that you live in, and see the light and joy of connection with other human beings; we would like to see you treat yourself with Reiki every day. If you have learned another form of healing that is not Reiki and you have been taught to treat yourself with it on a daily basis, then that is also acceptable. What we like up here about Reiki is that it has everything you need to join you to the rest of the universe. It is the universal life form energy collected and delivered to you by light beings that surround your planet. We are wholly present with this energy ourselves and recommend it. When you look for a Reiki Master for yourself to learn from, please ask us for help to lead you to a master who holds this energy in their body and aura fields. With our guidance you will not go wrong. Look for a master who treats themselves with Reiki daily.

Why all this emphasis on changing yourself first, why aren't you being told how to save the planet? I did say earlier about how to stop harming the planet and change your ways, and take these baby steps towards changing your own quality of light. Your light has the potential to shine brighter and brighter and be a beacon for others to follow. As a particle of All That Is, when you treat yourself you are connected to everything inside this universe; and you are treating everything inside this universe. Everything is God and God is everything. When I wrote that changing yourself is all that you can really do, it's a very powerful thing. That doesn't mean there aren't some more ideas.

7

THERE ARE THOSE of you who have been actively working as lightworkers for some time now. You have come to Earth now to do pre-selected jobs, chosen before you incarnated for this lifetime. You placed yourselves in the right positions to begin your work and some of you have thrown yourself into the work you chose. Others haven't done anything at all with their planned incarnations. You are all capable of so much. Every person alive here on the Earth at this time is capable of changing the world, for you are all splinters of one soul, equal to each other. That's why it's necessary for me to address all of you, I can't single out an elite. I acknowledge that some are more awake than others and ready to act, or are acting now on behalf of the planet. But you are all capable of getting the same results. Don't look at others and think you'll never be like them, for you could be like them tomorrow and surpass them the day after. It depends on how you accept new information.

Let's go back to the second section to the battle between light and dark. It's very real and part of your life here. If you are unable to see the dark angels and choose to ignore them they won't go away, they'll just carry on with their own methods of planetary control. They predate the start of your soul's residency here and are playing their role. If you choose to resist them wherever you find them you begin to wake up to the higher dimensions. It's not all fairies and light up there. It's going to take awareness that the motivation for some people's behaviour is darkness. When you go along with them even though you suspect that they are manipulating the situation so that the dark angels can rule, then you are acting like you are asleep and powerless. You are not powerless!

You all have the faculty of discernment, and the ability to tell light from dark and right from wrong. Something as ugly as dumping toxic waste in third world countries is being done in your name; are you happy about that? Do you think the next ten people you meet are happy about it? When you start to take tentative steps to say 'no, not in my name you don't', you will find you are not alone in your stance. All of these physical things I am talking about in my section carry an underlying energetic that is far greater than the single act of doing them. Suddenly you will have changed from a compliant, blind rabbit to a person with real strength, and you will be hard to pick off when the dark angels are looking for their own energy supply. But more than that you will be broadcasting some light into the darkness, and your light will show others what you are seeing. This has to begin somewhere.

The biggest challenges you are facing involve your environment and energy use. You still have enough bounty here to share between all of you and be comfortable, and to have enough to eat. But for some reason (which I hope you are starting to understand now), the Earth is being spoiled so that you will not be able to survive here *long enough to finish your game.* And if you fail to finish in a blaze of light together, the Earth can't go either. She of the shining beauty may end up dying.

Don't think that any of your small efforts are not worth making. You can't walk into someone's home on the other side of the world and turn down their thermostat, but you can turn down your own. It's all you need to do; these initial steps by those who care will start an avalanche of responsible living. It just needs to get going to build up momentum.

Unlike you, we can see what is going to happen when you all start to change, when you start saying 'no' to unsustainable living. There will come a day in a few years time when you will look back and say 'I can't believe we ever lived like that.' The Earth is stationary, poised at the point of turning her direction and snapping back like a rubber band. She has gone as far as she can in this direction. She must be allowed to recover or die. She votes for recovering.

8

I WANT TO GO back to the Earth healing circles in the section written by Melchizadek. If you want to start changing what is going on here I suggest this as your first activity. Take your friends and neighbours and begin your healing groups. It doesn't matter how often you meet or how many of you join in a circle, it is only important that you make a beginning. Those of you who know how to do Reiki or another suitable healing technique may start and those who don't can join in anyway. Their presence will strengthen the group and increase the flow of healing. It is recommended to have Reiki initiations for this work, but no one should be excluded. Don't have these circles without any healers of any kind; they should be based around the strength and knowledge of healers or people with Reiki.

Once you have made a beginning these circles will grow and become times of pleasure; there's nothing nicer than being connected and having the Reiki run through you for healing. We hope you will remember the music and food, and make a party of it. Joy is an aspect of love, too. Without joy you have not really connected to love, remember this when you go through your lives. We see too little joy here to carry the vibration of love strongly. Get used to being joyous.

The pleasure of the Reiki circles will increase your joy and love, which will change your own vibration as you walk on the Earth. This is how changes are made, of such simple things.

When you have set up your circles and are meeting old and new friends regularly you can take the circles farther by singing. This time of singing will not be like the music you listen to on radios, this will be different. When joy is expressed through song by a group it will be in joyful singing. More than that, when a group sings it binds itself together to become one. You are trying to become one, aren't you? For the time of singing you will be one. Children know this and love to sing in groups. When the singing is finished you will have sent the energy and vibration of your song out to the others on your planet, and to the planet itself. And to those who watch and feed on the vibration of misery, they will find nothing there they can survive on.

Imagine these circles occurring around the globe on a regular basis. It will look to us like the light from a series of campfires twinkling away, where the fires never entirely go out on the planet. This is how it was meant to be, there was always meant to be some light shining here in the darkness. The dark and the light were to show up in contrast to each other. The light from your circles is strengthening you as well as the planet, and it will show the planet that you actually do care about her. She needs to know that these days, as that is not her experience of hosting humans.

9

HERE IN THESE end days, the days before the great rebalancing waves of energy come through your sun to bless the Earth in 2012, you are feeling the energy of instability. Some of you may be afraid as you see the bedrocks of your society teetering, and dismayed to see the speed of change taking place in your lives. There is a widespread feeling of outrage that some through personal greed have put your own way of living at risk. From our point of view some of you are finally waking up and looking at the economic sustainability of your lifestyles. We are happy that the forces of chaos and corruption are making you look at how you live. We see the possibility of great alterations in how your societies live with each person forced to look again at how much of the Earth they are consuming each day. You may see it as deciding where and how you spend your money. This is an adjustment period to set the scene for the next phase.

The next phase will involve downsizing in many ways, but you will not be required to live in discomfort or hardship. You will find that some things are vastly improved in your newer, smaller homes that take so little to heat and run. There will be a rebalancing so that more of those on Earth have enough for their comfortable living. There does not need to be complete equality, but everyone requires enough for life. This is very far from the case now. When you think of how much you have, and how little some of the Earth's poorest people try to live on, then remember to look into their eyes and see yourself. You will treat others better because you see yourself in their eyes. That is the beginning of the coming together of human beings.

Those days will follow some of the hardest days you will have endured in your recorded history. There will be a good outcome, but many of you will learn the hard way how to make changes. This is nothing to be truly worried about, it will simply be rebalancing. You will need to see those days from the point of view of one soul, not the point of view of the many splinters. Sometimes what happens for the highest good is difficult to live through. We don't want you to worry about those days.

When you enter into the days of hardship and you are trying to make things better for yourself there are a few things you will still be able to do which will prove helpful. When everyone around you is struggling and at a loss to explain what is happening in their lives, you can still maintain your own balance. You maintain this through your connection with Reiki on a daily basis so that you are fed and supported through the universal life force energy. Also there comes a point with connection, and Reiki and love that dissolves fear and worry about the future. Living without fear and worry is living a completely different life from the past. Fear and worry are particularly useless emotions. We keep offering you Reiki over and over again, just as we did in Atlantis. We keep talking about it because when it is used daily it brings great change through connection with the Creator, the rest of the universe and love. If it is so strongly recommended by Archangels, why not try it? You don't actually need anything else, no secret rituals or spells or chants, just universal life force energy and love.

10

WHY DID WE just spend pages asking you to care for the Earth, and care for yourselves? Because we can see the timelines and possibilities for you and for the planet. We do not recommend many of you try to follow the tangle of lines that emanate from each moment. Imagine a tangle of wires coming out of the back of an old TV set; now imagine an infinite number of TV's with all their wires in a tangle. Do not believe seers on your planet, there in only one who is incarnate who can work through these wires, and that person sees the wisdom of not trying. Timelines can be unpredictable, and the farther you go into the future the less accurate you will be.

However we wish to go into the future ourselves in this part of this book, as we see clearly ourselves several main options for the next fifty years or so. We are not hampered by being incarnate or veiled, and we remember timeless space. We know that what looks like past, present and future to you is all only Now.

The three main scenarios are what we will lay out, but we wish to warn you that sometimes the most unlikely things happen!

11

SCENARIO ONE IS a planet with greatly increased desertification and the people and remaining animals confined to beltways of greenery. Perhaps thirty years or so from now the planet's population will have peaked and crashed with a massive death rate from lack of food and water. The death rate will be so high that there will be no one to bury the dead in many areas, leading to disease and further death, and fouled sources of water. Many of these deaths will be due to wars, which start with the largest countries on Earth and spread to the smaller ones. The surface of the Earth will be rocked with the explosions of fighting, which will carry on until the will to fight dies.

I do not need to tell you how much pain and hardship will be involved for humans and innocent animals in this scenario. When the fighting stops there will be a chance to start again with a vastly reduced population, as nowhere will be spared the wars and fighting. There will be crumbling and dangerous cityscapes, contaminated water and soil; some survivors will begin to farm again. Societies will reform and hatred and distrust will continue to flourish.

This scenario doesn't really have an end. This is the picture of a soul that continues its game in darkness while the death of the planet occurs under their feet. Until the final end of the universe humanity lives here in pain.

You may think I've put this picture in here just to scare you, but it is right there on one of your strongest timelines. You are so busy thinking up reasons to kill each other that you can't be surprised to see it here in print. I want to emphasize that this is very possible at this time. We would all feel better if you started to move in a different direction. We love this planet and don't want her to circle through the remainder of the ages left to this universe as a corpse.

This could happen and there is nothing we angels of light could do about it.

12

SCENARIO TWO IS more cheerful. After the war wipes out two thirds of humanity, you all begin to join together and say 'what were we thinking?' In the midst of sorrow you look around with eyes open, and understand exactly where your actions have led you. There is resolution in the hearts of the remaining people to live differently. By free choice you abandon those machines that led you to despoil the Earth, but you realise that you do not have to live like primitive cave men. There will be many good and renewable resources familiar to you that make your lives comfortable.

You realise that you have the opportunity to change and begin to repair the damage you have done the Earth; seriously repair all the damage you can wherever you can find it. All people join together in these projects of clean up and repair out of love for the planet. The balance between the new population level and the use of the Earth for farmland and fishing works better; there begin to be more fish in the seas, and more animals in the forests and jungles. The people are forced join together to make their lives work in communities that are sustainable and comfortable for all. Never again do they abuse the planet, animals or other life forms as they finally get the message and find respect for all others in their hearts.

As time goes by the human soul reaches out to its many fragments and starts to realise its own true nature as a thread in the tapestry of God. As all join together into one conscious soul they find their game is almost finished. As a last step they realise their relationship to the other life forms on this planet, solar system and the universe. All There Is, is a great community of existence of which humanity is a member.

The ascension of the human soul follows, and the Earth is left alive and well and able to choose her next step.

13

S CENARIO THREE. NARROWLY averting the worst death tolls in the wars, enough die to make people reconsider the futility of fighting and dying for someone else's ideas and gain. Soldiers refuse to raise their guns and fire at another human being, and they are sickened by what they have been asked to do. They lay down their weapons and go back home. When they are at home they remove from power all those who sent them out to kill their fellow humans and cause the death of so many of their own family and friends. The planet's population is reduced, but not as much as in the first two scenarios. Because of the damage to the infrastructures around the world the energy use is less and there is less travelling. People are forced to remember how to farm, and their contact with the Earth on a daily basis changes them further.

Bit by bit the society changes and becomes more sustainable and cleaner. The hold of the churches that war against each other is finally broken. Never again is heard the justification that it is a just and holy war, and that God is on our side against the others. It's still a hard world to survive in until many years later, when all is changed and cleaned up and people are adjusted to honouring the Earth again. When all changes have been made and the people are working with the planet, the crystal energy will be reintroduced. Once that happens people will be living in a society very far removed from the one that began the wars.

This is the quickest scenario for humanity finding their group soul, and that is why they lay their weapons down before killing everyone in the opposing armies; they see themselves in the soldiers fighting against them. In some ways this is the hardest scenario, for there will still be too many people living on the surface of the Earth and your efforts to rebalance will be harder. The demands for food and water will still be high enough to prevent an easy clean up and rapid repopulation of the planet with fish and animals. Your own coming together in love will help balance this out.

14

THERE IS SOMETHING we've been meaning to say in this book about your reproductive levels and the over-population of the Earth. We think you've stuck your head in the sand on this one. There are some of you who are replacing yourselves ten-fold with children, and at a time when the strain on resources is obvious to everyone. From the third world countries to the most prosperous ones, this is a trend that has not turned the corner yet. Your vast, swarming numbers are like locusts consuming all that the Earth can produce, and yet you are not the only species here. You leave nothing for anyone else. You have in Christian mythology a story of the Garden of Eden, a land of bounty where Adam and Eve could simply pluck their food and eat it. There is no implication of hard work in that story. The real work that they did was to look after the Garden and care for it as a whole, not just as a source of food for them. The food was food for all, and it was an honour to serve in the Garden to help it provide the food for all the other animals, birds, and insects. How did this story get twisted upside down so that all was put here to provide food for you? If you remove everything to do with universal love from this story you get the modern version.

When you think of losing all your modern comforts, you forget to think of losing all your modern discomforts. There has never been such a happy time for humanity since those early days when the Earth provided for you and your lives were blissful. Do not be afraid of changes, for not all change is bad.

15

S OME OF YOU will be worried that we mentioned wars and death in each of the most likely scenarios. This is an unhappy probability, an outcome of events that are building now. We want to reassure you that death is an ending, a pause, a break in your personal timeline. Death is not something to be feared, there is no hell waiting for you, but a continuation of your own soul on the other side. You will find yourself among friends and loved ones, swapping stories and studying the life you just completed. You will learn from all the experiences that you are having now. These experiences add up over the lifetimes that you are incarnate and leave you in a position to plan and organise your new lives, so that you can keep learning and understanding your own nature as part of the vast human soul. This soul absorbs the knowledge you bring to it after each lifetime. When you are living your lives here you do not have any access to this knowledge, but the knowledge is there. It's good the soul is learning, but this way is so slow for all of you.

The main point is that after you die there is peace and understanding and a continuation of you, but the better, wiser part of you. Without your bodies you do not have discomfort or pain, just a continuation of your own life, but up there in the higher dimensions instead of walking the Earth. It's a good rest time. Do not be afraid or worried.

When you next arrive down here for one of your lifetimes, you have in most instances arranged your family groups of mother, father and siblings. You've already found your future husbands and wives and your children. They've arranged your grandchildren for you. You have had long planning sessions together and have made some decisions about what you each want to get out of this new life. Then you're born and forget it all. But you have placed yourself with the people that you planned with, and most of the time you connect with your partners and children. Sometimes this fails to happen, but your higher self is on the job and guides you to new partners and often some of the same children. Then things start to happen to you and you begin to learn again about living your lives here. Many of the things you planned happen, a few never do. The important thing is that you chose to be here at the time you are here, having the experiences you are having.

There are a great number of you here right now who have come at this time to pick up a weapon and fight. When the day comes and the young men and women leave for battle do not grieve too much. Love them while they are with you now. I know this is hard to hear.

16

T HE BATTLES, WHEN they come, will be fierce. We have made arrangements that all of this fighting will be over quite quickly as the light will not benefit from long and drawn out fighting. The sooner it is over the more quickly the new world will begin, for better or for worse. If the young soldiers are able to stop their fighting, as in the third scenario, that will be the quickest resolution. There will be much destruction before the end of the fighting, with many cities and homes broken. There will be enough of everything for those who survive to live on, including companionship and joy.

This will be a very different world when humanity raises their eyes from their computer screens and electronic games and finds that they have real people to spend time with. The joy of working together for a common goal is experienced so infrequently now, and it seems always in the aftermath of some shared disaster. Have you really taken in what the Londoners were saying about the blitz in World War II? Why would they look back with longing at those dangerous days, except they were better than the days of peace that came afterwards in one important way? The separate splinters were joining together and finding they had so much in common. It was a time when people saw themselves in the eyes of others. It happened again in New York in 2001 when the World Trade Centre buildings fell. You don't need a disaster to feel this way. You only need understanding and love.

This is why we wanted to write this book, so that some of you would understand and *make a beginning*. Start the process and teach your children about treating others the way they would like to be treated themselves. Remember that one? It's older than the Bible. Look for yourself in the eyes of all you meet and you will not be able to harm them.

Sometimes when terrible things happen they have good results. Sometimes that's the only way to make real changes.

When is this war to be? We're not going to tell you, but it's fairly on its way now. It's been set in motion and the only way to avert it is to have an about-face in loving one another.

17

L ET'S TALK ABOUT something different. Let's talk about the year 2012, and the shift that we hope to see happening then. First, the energy will build during that year as waves of energy bathe the planet, so the effects and events we are talking about will have increasing energy behind them as the year goes by. There is no single, crucial moment or date; the date of 12-12-12 is too short to have everything happen on that day alone, all of a sudden. The energy will build toward that date, and things will happen all along, picking up speed and intensity as the months go by. When the 12-12-12 day comes we will consider it the end and stop the most intense parts of what is happening. I think everyone will need a little break by then, I know we will! We will wind down some energies after that, but it will just be the beginning for some things that are completely new and you will look back to that as their start date.

These few remaining years of 2009, 2010 and 2011 are important years of preparation. You will all have noticed the shake out of the greedy and immoral from your worldwide corporations, and the effect that has had on your economies. This was necessary to correct some serious imbalances in your money energy. Think of a green energy just as real as the gold of Reiki. This energy had been corrupted and had burst its natural boundaries; it was no longer a simple exchange mechanism. By rescuing the money and placing it back into context with the other energies present here on Earth a start was made to clean up and balance all the energy, and to remove it from the hands of those who were benefiting from its corruption. This was an unpleasant and shocking step for many of you, but it was necessary to make the correction now. As this most important correction feeds through the result will be fewer people who have more than they can ever spend, and fewer who never have enough to spend. The ends need to be brought closer to the middle.

Because we began with the money we are on schedule to have that part of the correction finished in the year 2012. A correction does not mean everything will be as it was before the stock markets fell, it means it will be healthier and in correct balance. You will have new foundations for your world economies to build on. These will be real foundations made of real items that can be exchanged for money and not something artificial made up and sold by corrupt men. You don't know how long it's been since your economies had these foundations, but I would go back hundreds of years before anyone had captured any other countries and taken their wealth from them. Standing on your own two feet and trading something real in goods or services with others will in the end be just as profitable as, and more pleasant than, what you have been used to. So that will be a good thing, and the adjustments are happening quickly. If you think of this as your goal, then don't try to prop up anything that doesn't fit this pattern.

The economy being set on quicksand, on a false and unsupportive bottom allowed it to explode into a vast bubble of nothingness. You will feel something different energetically when this has come to rest on a real bottom. The energy will feel solid, and a little old-fashioned. The attention will be taken away from money, which is after all only a tool for you to use for your own convenience in exchange, and put back onto all the other things that a society is made up of. It will go back onto production and goods and services; crops and arts. More people will support the societies you live in, because they are not excluded by not having enough money. The operas will still be performed, but the tickets will cost less and more people will come and enjoy the music. These things will continue without a few very rich people to support them. All that has value will remain, and those showy things of no worth will vanish. It will be easier to see what is genuine with less in your way, and fewer distractions.

When stocks are offered for sale on the stock market to raise capital for a business it will be because they are making something that people want to invest in. In your recent past very, very few shares were sold for this reason. Shares were sold on the idea of being a safe financial investment that would go up and make money quickly for the buyer. Share sales in the future will go back to educated investors who understand the markets thoroughly and have given up on speculation. That is a legitimate use of the stock markets, and the markets will once again be steady and a good place to keep some of your money. They are entering into this period now and in the next two to three years will have new foundations to build upon. We have stepped into the global stock markets and our presence of light will heal what has been happening there. Let your worries go about your stock market investments.

Those other great bastions of darkness, the great global banks, will not exist in their present corrupt forms either. After the rotten apples have been shaken down from the trees, the banks will go back to borrowing and lending money as banks should. It will take a long time for them to be trusted again. These huge banks that served as money making machines for the few at the expense of the many were your temples of money, where only money had value and people outside the banks were ignored and treated with very little respect. There is no further use for this kind of attitude in a world where you see yourself in the eyes of all you meet. Let them go.

Where are you going to make money, or invest your money for income? Look at a world without financial instruments and what is left; a whole world full of opportunities. Take your investment money and study and find somewhere to put it yourself. Who could really use the money and give you a return on it, and does the return have to be financial? There are those who can return something to you for your cash that is not more money; such as services, or supporting an artist, or helping someone in their life, or a scholarship for someone just starting out, or a manufacturer or farmer who can expand or improve their business. Wrench your gaze away from what you knew, that narrow band of investments, and turn it onto everything else. You're not used to doing this anymore, but you used to support each other in this way in the past. Don't be afraid to support each other again.

18

I N TWO TO THREE years you will have changed the energy of money and finances into solid, practical light. That will have a knock-on effect on almost all other aspects of your lives. You all have and use money; there's usually money in your pockets. Now the money will be made of light instead of darkness, and it will be so much harder to abuse. You will respectfully hand over cash to farmers and others that are in a necessary partnership with you, with a feeling of gratitude for what they do. Maybe this will be enough to reform your modern agriculture; we'll see. Your farmers are not valued and respected enough for the important work they do for all of the rest of you. There is a core of unhappiness in this group that feeds through into the food you eat. They are a group of people who need something back from you in gratitude and acknowledgement, and if you can alter their energy, the energy of your food will change. It does you no good to eat food that is grown without love, respect and gratitude, and I'm talking about the plants and animals here.

This is one common area of your lives that you can change now by taking your focus off yourself and facing towards your food producers. Inform yourselves as to the manufacturing processes of your modern foods. Follow them from their chemical-laden beginnings to their over-processed ends. Ask yourselves why you would choose to eat such food, and what you expect the results to be. You are dealing with an epidemic of malnutrition from the richest to the poorest countries, and all the painful health problems associated with it.

Now go back to your farmer and see what you could do to help him grow his food organically. When he stops spreading tons of chemicals on his fields there will be an end to some of the poisoning of your land and water. When we talked about cleaning up the Earth earlier, we certainly meant this to be part of the clean-up. This 'invisible' chemical pollution is the largest polluter of the countryside worldwide. It affects all life from human to insect that lives in your crop growing areas, and it affects your own food. It would be a start to change this now by buying

117

organically grown food, or perhaps combining with others to guarantee to buy organic food from a local grower so they knew what to plant and grow. Help them to help you.

The food you have been eating has been significantly altered over the last one hundred years, and the new epidemics of ADHD, asthma, heart disease, diabetes and cancer are made worse by your modern eating habits. This makes you increasingly turn to pharmaceutical drugs for your medication and health. There are many drugs out there that have little beneficial effect compared to a healthy diet made up of fresh organic foods. The drug companies are not your friends; they are profit-making organisations that depend on a steady supply of sick people for their existence. The responsibility for your own health is yours, and there is much you can do with food and exercise that will make you stronger and healthier. When illness or accidents happen, let your medical industry be there as a back up to your natural good health.

Finally, when you realise the toxicity of many of your common lifestyle habits, from pouring bleach into toilets to mass chemical spraying from aircraft over fields of crops; please can you stop? Seriously, buy some greener products the next time you shop. Many good products are there on the shelves now, and as I said earlier you can only change what you do yourself, not what someone else does.

19

B Y THE BEGINNING of 2012 some of you will have made significant steps towards bringing down your carbon footprints and that will make a difference to what begins to happen during that year. The physical acts of change have to go hand in hand with the energetic; not only will it be easier for those who have made changes to live with the new energy, but their new energy will influence everyone around them.

The energy coming to the Earth will alter and affect some people differently than others. It will be easiest for those who have been working with the light to walk through the year comfortably. It will be easier for the Earth if there has been some attempt made to clean her and look after her. This incoming energy is for her; at a prearranged time she is being given her own help to begin her own process of ascension. This will be a series of powerful waves of crystalline energy from the centre of the universe where the Source of all is. When you want to go through the walls of the universe to find timeless space, go to the centre.

When these waves begin to arrive for the Earth she will begin her transformation by 'shaking loose', quivering to get rid of the old energy and replacing it with new. It is a very big deal for her, which she has long anticipated. This is her energy exchange, her old energy will leave and be replaced by new, and she will be a 'new Earth' in energetic terms. We will help her through this process, and hold her with love while she transforms herself. She will then wait transformed, for you to be ready.

What does that mean to all of you living on her back like fleas? She will need to quiver and vibrate under the influence of the new energy, and she won't be able or wish to stop it. It will have a smaller effect on people as the energy is not pitched at you. Those of you who have already raised your vibration through Reiki or other healing methods will feel it pass through your bodies and purify you also. You and the Earth will purify and unload darkness and toxins together. When this was all arranged a long time ago no one knew that the Earth would be so poisoned and toxic when this energy started to come through. We have some concerns about what we see happening in 2012.

She has a lot to shake off and it will start as shaking in the higher dimensions, at a higher and faster rate. It will eventually come down to shaking in the lower dimensions or your physical Earth. Those of you who are closest to her higher vibration will feel this least. When more of you hold light in your physical and energy bodies, and the more light there is on her surface, the easier it will be for her and all of you. This is going to be a point when you are balancing her, steadying her. Imagine a shaking floor where those who don't shine any light are falling over, but you are there steadying the floor yourself with your own light. Now you can start to see that being a figure of light yourself and practising your Reiki every day, will change you and change your planet.

Steadying and balancing this planet will affect all of you so much because you live here on top of her. The potential for earthquakes is certainly increased during this time in many places. Help her to be gentle. Remember the generosity of a planet that was prepared to give you the Garden of Eden with all you needed for life. This planet is not out to harm you now, she needs your help. How severe some of this earthquake activity can be influenced by you following the steps covered in the earlier sections.

2012 is going to be an eventful year for you. We can see that there are variables that have been introduced that affect what will be taking place. Holding on to the idea of a better world, and working together to clean up your planet, big businesses, agricultural practices and relationships with other humans will make a huge difference to how the year ends. Practising your Reiki every day, forming healing circles and caring for the Earth in an energetic way will be the other side of this story. When 2012 comes you can reel along like drunks falling all over the place, or walk steadily as caretakers and helpers. This is a time for individual choice and action, before 2012.

20

WHEN 2012 BEGINS and you are all excitedly waiting for the new energy and new events to take place and perhaps some will be talking about the end of the world according to the Mayan calendar, remember that even now the events of that year are not set in stone. The Mayan calendar refers to a universal cycle of energy, and it correctly predicts the return of that energy in 2012. When that energy hits here the Earth will want it to soak in, for the help and healing it brings. It's a bit like planetary food. Right now you have such a layer of black, tarry energy on most of the planet that the energy will *go around, and slide off.* There is much to do to lift and dissolve this blackness, to open spaces where the energy will soak in.

In this book so far we have given you techniques that all of you can use to change what is happening here on the surface of the Earth. The largest and fastest changes will take place as you find in your hearts more love to share with others, human and non-human on this planet. You can use Reiki to help you and help the planet. If you help yourselves become less dark, the planet will benefit. You can spend time and money on cleaning up the planet, all the little corners of sadness as well as the big scars. Start close to home and work outward. That will be the quickest way to cover the ground with light. Clean up and then use Reiki or another healing system on the scars. It looks like an insurmountable job for a few, but if there are many it won't take as long. The cleaning allows the light to reach the surface of the Earth itself, and it will get the energy it needs.

When some of you meet in groups for meditation you have been practising a form of grounding that uses the Earth to anchor you. We would like to point out that this is not necessary. I would like to recommend that you practice grounding yourself all day long as follows: be present in your lives. Wherever you are and whatever you are doing be present and focused. This is the opposite of daydreaming or being distracted. When you are present you are "in the now", and that is being grounded in yourself and not the Earth. Spare her this one little job and learn to be grounded all day long and in balance through your own efforts.

We are all hoping that by the time you have read this book you will be able to look at various practices and see the hand of the dark angels and how they have infiltrated all of your lives. By looking at the effect of your actions we hope you will see more clearly and choose the light. We realise you did not know, that you are blind and can't see them as we do, but you are being informed now. Please use the information I have given you to make a start, to show your new intentions by beginning to clean up the planet, heal the Earth, and heal the human soul. We are here to help you do that.

With great love for all of you,
Ariel

Section Five

Possible Futures for Planet Earth

ARCHANGEL OF TRANSFORMATION

1

MY NAME IS ESMARIEL and I am the Archangel of Transformation. My role in ancient Atlantis brought forward the energy for change. I am not the only angel who can help with change, but the way I help is by transforming energy into matter, and matter into energy. I am an angel from the Void, and from the timeless space between the universes I have come with the raw creative energy that originally produced the universes. When I am present in your universe I have enough energy to spark transformation, by working with those who ask for my help. I have come here now to your planet because she is very close to her time for transformation. She has called me and I have come.

In the beginning I came here to help the human soul transform themselves into physical beings, following their wish and contract with the planet. It was an exciting time, the beginning of this new, extreme game. You wished to make your energy into matter, and become present here in biological bodies, so I facilitated your transformation. I also helped the Earth become the paradise she wished to become. For me to be involved in the games in these ways is to use my skills and act as my role has been devised. It is very satisfying for me, and for this game I was working with the beautiful being that is your planet, a great favourite with us all. She is such a loving and sparkling soul.

After a while I returned here again to answer her call, and saw the gaping wounds on her surface from the human activities during the fourth age of Atlantis. This was heart-breaking to me, and when it was explained that she was asking for that entire continent to be removed whole I was filled with sadness for her. What she was asking was similar to one of you cutting into your own bodies and ripping out a major organ. I understood her request and when the archangelic collective acted on her behalf my role was to transform the hole to seabed and ocean. I raised the physical matter of the land into the purely energetic continent it is today in the higher dimensions, as we did not need to wipe from existence part of herself, just remove it into her energy fields where it still exists, but not as physical land. This has altered her energy fields a lot (!), where there were smooth layers intermingling and flowing freely, swirling together and blending, there was now a great big continent stuck in the way, and there was trauma remaining from the removal of Atlantis. From that day to this, the health of this planet has been damaged by the restriction in her energetic flow; the energy does not flow the way it should for her best health. She no longer has all her native strength to cope with everything that has been done to her by you and the dark angels.

The fact that Atlantis still exists in the memory of the human race is due to its presence in her higher dimensions. The higher dimensions are a storehouse of knowledge for you that you access through your dreams and channelling, and sometimes just knowing. Some of you are more open and find it easier to remember than others, and that is why some find it easier to access the information held around the Earth. This knowledge is the Akashic records, a record of almost all that has happened here. Akashic readers are those who can read what is written there. There is much that you can learn now from these records.

When Atlantis had been transformed into energy there was a great crisis here, the planet was so wounded we angels of light were busy for a long time trying to patch up and balance her again. She was like a coma patient with a drip and we were feeding her, she was not able to draw in her own light. She eventually almost balanced, and there she stayed spinning a little out of control and using her energy and ours to do what should have come naturally; maintain her own equilibrium.

This situation is now ready to end for her. She will be complete once more if she is able to ascend, as she will be a new being of light at that time. She will discard her imbalances and reabsorb Atlantis into the whole. Replacing Atlantis into the Atlantic Ocean will happen on an energetic, not a physical level, and that wound will heal at long last. Earth won't vanish from beneath your feet into a cloud of gas, she will still be here and she will wait out your game but in an advanced state of consciousness. Her final ascension will happen as the game ends, not while lives are depending on her. All life will have to go together, human, animal, plant and more. That will be a happy day for everyone concerned. Your consciousnesses will have all joined together at that time with the Earth's and you will go as one indivisible life form.

What does that remind you of? Remember the description of the universe being made up of tiny pieces of the Creator so that he could learn about himself? This is a planet-sized section coming back together as part of the tapestry of God. You will be more than a thread, perhaps you may be a small corner section. You will not separate again until the end of the universe itself. You will be God-realised, you will know that you are God and will move on to play further from a position of knowing, and as you understand the nature of God you will play with these other souls *as one*. For you are all one now, you're just having a little trouble remembering that part.

2

D O YOU KNOW what it is like to transform yourselves? Some of you are very good at transformation at an individual level. We have watched with admiration the efforts many of you make to change yourselves and look for happiness in so many different ways by talking to psychologists, using Reiki and other therapies. You still know that you want to be happy; you haven't forgotten that in all these years. As you approach joy and the darkness drops away from you, you approach the Creator from a position of light and bliss. This is where we marvel when we watch you, and choose to help you with all our hearts. You chose such a hard path, and it has been so painful for so long but you reach out to each other and help.

We have witnessed changes in humanity, enormous changes even in the last two hundred years. Back then the slave trade was coming to an end in Britain through revulsion at the inhuman treatment that was suffered by some at the hands of others. Slavery is tiny on this planet now compared to what it used to be. We hope to see this finally come to an end soon. If it's tolerated in your society, what does it say about you? And there are other examples of goodness and kindness shown to each other, and the feeling among a good many of you that you can't treat another as if they are not human. You have chosen to fight for the victimised and persecuted, and tried to rescue and save where you can. These are not the actions of a soul that is lost to darkness. This is a soul of light we see when we look at you. Don't let your natural brightness and search for joy be sidetracked by dark entities riding on your shoulders. Push them off; they have no right to be there.

3

NOW THAT YOU know how we see you, we would like you to cheer up, be happy, find joy and bring light and love into your lives. There will be no room for anything else to stick to you when you have surrounded yourself this way. Also you will not be providing food for these dark entities; you'll have put them on a starvation diet. This is transformation; from 'I'm not sure where I'm going' to 'I choose light and love.' And if you ask me to help you, I will. I could turn an idea into reality at the beginning of the game, and I can help you again now. It's what I do; my talents and energy do exactly that.

When you wish for me to help you transform yourself, say "Esmariel, come to my assistance. I am ready now to change." I will be there and the energy for change will be unstoppable; it is a one-way flow to something new and there is no turning back. I hope that many of you will look at your lives and ask for help, and are not afraid of a future that is made of love and light. Remember that you are able to create the future you want, and my energy will assist you to do just that. I can see the potential futures that are waiting for you as individuals, and as a single soul. Do not be afraid to walk with me into the light.

The changes that come to you with my help will be the changes that you need for happiness, and they will come in the right amount and at the right time for you to cope with and benefit from. I have gentleness and care for you that would not accept any other way of change. On the other hand there are some of you who are ready to accelerate like rockets, and your pace of change will be very swift. You wouldn't want to take it any slower and you will change very quickly. Some of you who read this book will have started changing at the previous paragraph, and some will wish to think and wait. As the numbers of people increase who are ready to transform and choose light, a head of steam will begin to build up towards a very dramatic shift of values, attitudes and behaviour. Today you can't imagine anyone giving up their 4 × 4 car just to save the planet, tomorrow no one will want to own one because of the carbon footprint it has. Change is a wonderful thing, and I'm here to help you go with the flow of energy that is change.

You look at all the change needed and some of you feel despair, and you don't know how you are going to drag everyone else with you on the path to saving the planet. Some people live so far away on the other side of the world and you think even if you change that they never will. They will change more quickly if the energy of change is irresistible, if your own rate of change is causing a flow and movement. The movement of energy is *everything*; it is stagnation you want to get rid of. When you begin to change the energy of transformation is freed up and turned loose and that is exactly how change happens.

Now, what is change exactly? What is the most powerful, irresistible force present in the universe? Some will be thinking love, but it is change. The drive for change is overwhelming and constant. When someone says "go with the flow", they refer to not resisting change, and allowing it to take place in you, around you, and through you. You only really have a problem when you try to keep things as they are. Let everything slide through your hands and enjoy it for the moment you are holding it. Something else will be there to replace it the second it is gone. Only by enjoying the flow of change will you leave behind your sorrow that things and people you loved are gone. Enjoy all that comes your way and let excitement and the unexpected into your lives.

There are some of you who are trying so hard to preserve your lives and society and your personal belongings. You have shut out energy from your lives. It is dancing past you and tugging at you, but you have your heads down and your arms are full of your possessions and you won't let anything go. But you will not be able to resist the movement of the energy forever. So much energy of your own can be expended in trying to resist the flow of my energy, and you fail to see that what is coming is better than what you have. You give up contentment to hold onto valueless possessions. It is such a stagnant life.

My goal is this, as the Archangel of Transformation I would see everyone on the planet let go of their fears about change. Fear is food for the dark angels, and stagnation and fear suit them very well. Next I would see people ask me for help so the cool breezes of change begin to flow through lives one by one. After a while there would be more who were relaxed and welcoming of new ideas and ways of living. The energy of change would begin to touch everyone whether they were afraid of it or not, and as their neighbours transformed so would they. Energy circles the globe faster than anything manmade and as the breezes picked up into strong winds they would reach the other countries that you are worried will never want to change. Change is in the air, as they say.

How do you save the world and change everyone – change yourself. Allow the change to happen to you, all the transformation you need is here now in my presence. When you decide to change and ask me for help the process is started. The rate of change, and the manner of changes you choose to make may surprise you.

4

WHAT CHANGES WOULD you each like to see take place? This is where you are the most powerful; when you start to choose the world you would like to live in. Let's say one of you chooses clean air and water from a position of knowing that as a part of the Creator he or she has all the power necessary to make it happen. This choice would be followed by a clean-up where you humans change the way you live and clean up the planet. It would come about as choice followed by change of habits, and cleaning up. Why not just zap the planet clean as God? This would not be in line with the universal law of cause and effect, put into place as part of the rules of this universe. You're going to have to do the work on this one. Get together with others and make a start.

The way to begin this process is to let go of the reluctance to change, ask for my help, and watch and see what begins to happen in your life. Let go of any ideas or possessions that you have outgrown or are stagnant and going mouldy in your life. Allow the new energy to swirl you into a new place where you are re-energised and change is happening. Some will change by staying in their homes and jobs, but becoming very different people. Others will pick up and move away to their new perfect home. Wait and see. If you knew that you could be extremely happy in a new job in a new place to live, would you want to give that up and stay where you are? Because staying stagnant is giving up everything you might have had if you were free to accept the gift you were prepared to give yourself. From my perspective, staying stagnant is the way to lose everything, and letting everything go is the way to gain everything of value in your lives.

We Archangels are team members of the Archangelic Collective, and if you let the message of Ariel in the last chapter motivate you to help the Earth and wish to change your own habits, then I am here to give you the jump-start to do exactly that. We are here out of love for the Earth and you, your soul matters to us too. We watch you struggling, like swimmers in a race who don't have any idea where the finish line is and are swimming in a jumbled-up mob. As in Atlantean times we are still here to help you, but you have not heard our voices for a long time now. We care about you.

We are putting into motion our plan now to help you and help the Earth. We are instructing you in this book so that you will know more about how the universe really works and who you and the planet are, what has been happening here, and how you can reverse what has been happening. It is our wish and desire to help you change, and help set up the Earth for her ascension, which will in turn set you up for yours. As has been said before, you all go together. Reading this book is not enough; we are looking for you to wish to transform yourselves and your actions and we are here to help you. When you choose to change yourself, everything will begin to change. *Everything* will begin to change. And that's when the fun will really begin again.

5

A LONG TIME AGO in the early days of Atlantis you actually led very happy lives, from cradle to grave. Let's go back to the Garden of Eden story, but have more people living in the Garden. Your lives were blessed with easy food, so you didn't have to work to grow anything in fields; you just picked it from its growing place. You had speech, music and dance, theatre and entertainment, pleasant and happy companions. We walked among you and helped you to connect to the outer universe so you could connect with God and his energy. There was no need for you to work for anything. You looked the same as you do now in this, your chosen physical form. You were happy, all day and every day. It's a wonder the dark angels ever found a toe-hold here to change you into the unhappy people you are now.

Compare that picture to how you live now with your separation, your stress and hard work. Some of you work so hard you die young, all worn out. We who remember your happy past feel so sorry for you now. It is not so many years since women have stopped having baby after baby until they also died young. You never used to reproduce at such a rate, reproduction out of fear that there would be no one to look after you in your old age. You used to have just enough children, one, two or sometimes three in the case of twins being born. You were such good friends with them, and you knew them better than anyone else and enjoyed their company the most. Your population was stable and everyone was looked after. No one was alone, or left alone to care for babies or the elderly as it was done in community. The days were filled with talking and singing together, the nights were quiet under the many stars visible in the sky. You lost all this, and you gained a delusion, a promise of more instead of enough. But you didn't know it would be more unhappiness, and not enough joy.

Can the human race ever go back, ever live a life deeply happy as it was in the past? What would you say if we said yes? I am going to show you three different versions of your future, three possible futures that you could end up living in the not too far distant future.

6

IN THE FIRST possibility there are fewer people, and the Earth is being cared for again. Where there were ugly sores left from old building sites, landfills and toxic dumps there is now greenery and health. Place by place decisions were made about how to restore the health of each corner of land. Lakes and rivers are being cleaned and car parks are broken up to let the sunlight back onto the ground. Where everything has been cleaned the energy has changed from death to life, and the plants grow once again with ease. The life-giving energy has returned to the food supply and people are benefiting from the cleaner air and water, and they feel more alive themselves.

In order to bring about these changes they gave up some of their most harmful habits. They banished petrol driven vehicles, but suddenly there was a new, clean fuel for transportation. They wished still to travel and see their friends and the beautiful world and their desires were granted. (Who chose to create that fuel?) Most people spend a fair number of hours a week growing food, for this is a transition phase involving farming. Their food plots are not farms, but are smaller and close together like English allotments. There is camaraderie, and the old teach the young. The young are too involved and busy to gang together and do nothing; they see their friends while they are busy helping and working. They know they are valued as part of the family and society.

The houses and town centres are smaller, and the shops sell only those things that are actually useful for life. The houses are warm and comfortable, and are powered cleanly. Big power stations are not needed for the smaller population. Instead the power supply is more local, and people settle near to where they can produce power cleanly and naturally. Energy is not wasted trying to power it along lines to far distant corners of the country. When night falls the lights come on and there is still communication through electronic means and telephones. Cooking is in ovens and the water is running indoors to the sinks. Houses will be smaller so they do not require so much heat or cooling and they take advantage of trees for summer shade and winter windbreaks.

What's missing here for your happiness? There may be some small extras, but the main things are here to keep a family happy. There are many in your world today who would consider themselves very blessed to live a life in these communities. This kind of community is the kind that lets you live in happiness, without the joy-destroying stress of your modern ways. Some of you have so many possessions you have difficulty caring for them all, and some have too little for life. That is you, your own soul who is starving over there. This way there is enough for all.

7

THERE IS A second future possibility I can show you that takes place some years later on from the one above. The families are living in warm and comfortable homes but the small croplands have vanished. Instead there are food plants near every house, encouraged to grow nearby originally; now they are there and need very little care or attention. The homes are set in pleasant gardens with food and flower plants, trees and shrubs. The food still needs to be picked and prepared, some needs to be put away and stored for the winter and the whole family makes sure this is done. There is much socialising as there is always enough time to visit friends. A couple or family may walk down to friends who live next to a river and come away with fish for supper, or visit the woman who makes such beautiful pots to trade for a new one with something they've preserved. The days of the man leaving home to work all day have been given up; no man wants to work as hard as they did in the past. They still see their men friends for social time, just as the women still get together with their women friends.

The homes have returned to crystal energy as their energy source. There is no lack of energy to run a kiln or charge up the small transport cars or fliers for longer journeys. The communicator crystals have returned and now they are used instead of phones to stay in touch and email has vanished as being too cumbersome.

People have started to live longer now that they work with less stress, and their food is fresh and wholesome. That means they live next to their parents, and later their children, grandchildren and great-grandchildren. There is joy at the closeness they have found with their families and communities.

Sometimes when people are out travelling in the countryside they meet with some other residents of this planet, the elementals. It's always a treat and a thrill to be shown something new by a centaur or wood elf. Although they do not choose to live together there is friendship as they are all committed to looking after the Earth. The earlier toxic dumps have now been dealt with, and she has been healed of her wounds and scars. The elementals were the ones who helped with the final solutions to some of the worst destruction, and they joined with you to heal the Earth.

Animals have increased their numbers once again and are making their own lives in the spaces between the villages. They rarely come into contact with you, except for some who choose to, and it is no surprise to see dogs and cats among the ones living with you. Gone are the days when vast numbers were raised and sent through slaughter houses for your meals. These animals can finally get on with their own games they contracted for when they approached the Earth for a home. People do not get in their way but allow them to live their lives with respect. One day, when more people are ready there begins to be a blend of the human and animal consciousness and a beginning is made towards all being one together.

What is different about this picture is the contentment of those who are living at this time, whether human or animal, insect or plant. They have found a way to live in love and harmony with each other and it makes them stronger. They do not feel they are missing anything, and everyone has enough.

This is a possible future, not a guaranteed future.

8

HERE IS A third possible future for all of you. Years have gone by after the above times. People are regularly connecting telepathically where before it was just some people, some of the time. There are some extended families that are very good at this and they have joined their consciousnesses together as a mini-human-consciousness, and are using it as a method of learning as other souls do. Those families are very successful at living as their communication skills make everything easier. When berries are ready to pick they all know at once as soon as one has found them, and are able to go and pick them. It is the same with everything. As they marry with others and spread out more people understand how the telepathy works and it increases in use. Sharing their consciousness really makes them understand that they are one.

Some lead the way as they start to blend with the animal and insect consciousness, the plants and others. There are living beings that have consciousness that you have never dreamed were alive and conscious.

Once the whole human population has joined back into one human consciousness their part of the game is over. There will be a small space while they get ready to join with all life, and then everyone goes together and your game is finished. You, the planet and all life here will become one new, large soul to sing your own song in the universe. And that is what is so different really about this game, for in order to accept such a dangerous game on her surface the Earth asked for a greater payment at the end. Her charge to you as the human soul, her payment request was that you would join her at the end of the game and become one. She wished to take a step closer to the point of coming back together to reassemble as God and you were willing to help her do that.

Now do you see why this one game has such a large effect on the rest of this universe? If you are taking a step towards returning to the Creator, then the separation has ended and the return has started. It will be an event that catalyses the rest of the universe to draw together and

139

return. It will reverse the energy flow, and there is nothing more important than energy flow.

I am the Archangel of Transformation, and I cannot think of a greater transformation than reversing the expansion of the universe and starting the process of returning to God. This is why I am here now. Do not forget the first of Ariel's scenarios where the planet stagnates into darkness. That possibility is a very real one yet. Do you wish to end like that, or would you prefer to find joy, and ultimately rejoin your Creator through bliss? It's up to you. When you choose to work with me I will help you find these futures I have described. They are all there ahead of you if you set your feet on the right path.

These possible futures follow Ariel's descriptions of war. If you do not have the war or if you do not have a hard enough war the futures will be slightly different. Sometimes the path that looks the hardest and is the one to be avoided at all costs is actually the one that takes you to the right place. I'm sorry to speak again about a war, but we see it as a war of light and are looking beyond it to the end results. You will find it difficult to prevent now.

9

IWOULD LIKE TO say something about the post-2012 world, the world where enough of you have changed and anchored light into the planet. You will find something different in the air in those days following the wind down of the energy waves. First, the Earth itself will have changed, she won't look different at first but she will have changed on the inside. Her cobwebs will have been blown away and she's going to be feeling like she is back in control after a long illness. There will be a spring in her step as she sails around the sun. Her return to health will affect the rate at which she is able to heal herself of her sores and wounds on the outside, and that is what you will notice first. You will be surprised at how the seasons regulate, and the rainfall becomes more regular and beneficial. The winters will be colder to help those areas that are supposed to be frozen, like the Arctic and Antarctic, the tundra and permafrost areas. No more melting there! It will come just in time to prevent some terrible natural disasters due to melting ice. Some of your scientists have predicted the shifting of the Gulf Stream and the freezing of Europe, as well as the death of wildlife dependent on snow and ice. There are still some timelines showing these futures.

As the planet gets her strength back, stops reeling, settles down and remembers what it is like to be well, she will gradually balance her orbit. She is not going to tip back suddenly and shock everyone, although that is exactly what she planned to do not too long ago. She has decided to slowly, imperceptibly straighten up. We recommend that you watch and keep records that you can measure over long spans of time to see this happening. One day when she is upright again she will feel better, and you will have slowly adjusted to the changing pattern of the seasons. Balance and predictability will help all of you to grow enough to eat for your population size. There will be more food for the animals and insects also.

So when is the war going to be? The warning signs will be the intractability of the world religions who decree their followers must fight and die to prove their God is the strongest. It will be a war of religion, and you will see it coming. It's up to you what you do when it's here. At that time we will not step in to stop it.

Those first years when the Earth is healing is when you will begin to see her people once more. There are so many elementals here working as servants and helpers of the planet, some you would think of as gardeners, but there are so many kinds with so many jobs that they do. They have their own roles and own lessons to learn, they have their own contracts and games to complete running side by side with yours. You used to be able to see them, but it is a rare person now who does; mostly children and people who have an open mind and third eye. These friends are the first you will begin to see again. They don't have any problem seeing or hearing you. When the sighting of fairies and dragons and all the rest become more common you will know that some of the veil is lifting at last. These compatriots are here in the fifth dimension, we hope you will adjust your sight quickly to see the first five dimensions so that you can learn to live with the others more easily. You have the lower three dimensions and they fit naturally in with the next two.

As I mentioned earlier, these are the beings that will be able to show you how to clean up some of your worst messes. Who better to show you how to look after trees than a dryad? They're waiting to help you, and looking forward to the days you will work together. They are beings of light in their way, but not of the same kind of light that angels are made up of. We are different, and we both serve the light. They are spread across the universe serving the planets, and staying with their chosen planet. We do not stay at one planet; we visit every planet from time to time and come when we are called. We can be at more than one planet at a time, as time is irrelevant to us, it doesn't exist.

Your elementals have had a pretty hard time of it since you arrived wearing your blindfolds. Until the time of your game they were partners with the previous souls living here. Your inability to see them prevented you from working with them. Then the planet became overrun with dark entities and their anti-elementals (we have elementals of light, they have ones of dark that harm where the light ones heal.) The planetary helpers were left with too much to do, they did everything they were able, but in many areas there was more work than they could possibly handle. In some areas they were either non-existent or pretty thin on the ground. The more of the dark entities there are; the fewer ones of light in that area. Their kingdoms thrive in the wild countries best, magical places that feel different and special. That's where they have been able to preserve a bit of the Earth as it should have been all this time.

If you look again at the Narnia books by C S Lewis you will find a country where the fauns, gnomes, dwarfs and others are part of the kingdom, all equals with the talking animals and men. They are the free peoples of Narnia, where none is a servant to another and the land is treated well. These are children's stories, but like so many of your fiction writers there is the truth of your possible world showing through. You could live in a happy world like Narnia yourself one day, but it will only be after you have made it that way. Meanwhile, think about all those elementals that you could be seeing, but you're not seeing now. They could be part of your life and community, and we hope they will be one day.

10

I AM COMING NEAR to the end of my section now, and I have one last subject to cover. There are those of you who can already see and hear quite a lot that you keep quiet about. You are afraid of the reaction of those around you who can't see or hear as you do, and often with good reason as they've mocked you in the past. No one likes to be made fun of, I know. It's time to stick your neck out a little again, and say what it is you can see. Point it out to show others around you and describe it, and if they can't see it just shrug and say "oh, you can't see that moving over there?" Don't give up; there are as many out there who would love to be taught, as many as there are that would laugh. Sightings are more likely to take place out of the city centres.

You will see more and more movies and books that feature this magical world, and that's because we are inspiring those movies and books. Go ahead and believe, and learn from them. Think, "am I supposed to be getting a message here?" In your Bible you had Old Testament prophets giving their messages of God, but here we use mass media because we want to reach as many of you as we can. Those who are actively looking can learn a lot this way. Some messages are pretty simple, others more complex. Learn what you can. You can ask for help if it seems that you can't quite grasp something that seems significant. We're having quite a bit of fun with this new media.

Your great prophets of the modern age that we inspired are JRR Tolkien, and C S Lewis. Go back to the books if you want to find out what we wanted you to know. Don't forget the Silmarillion by Tolkien. Favourite movies are Inkheart, Stardust, and Enchanted to name some recent ones. The first series of Heroes had a lot of input as did movies about the X-Men. You have the ability to be so much more than you are now, for you have dormant skills.

I am Esmariel, Archangel of Transformation, lady of the pink flame. It is my time here again, a time of change and transformation. Call on me when you are ready to let go and move on. The more that do this, and the earlier they ask, will bring about change from fear and unhappiness to new lives of contentment. You are good people, and we are all here to help you finish your game in an explosion of light.

Section Six

A Message of Hope for Humanity

ARCHANGEL HOPHRIEL, ANGEL OF HOPE

1

M Y NAME IS HOPHRIEL, and I am the Archangel of Hope. I come to you at the end of this book to show you a picture of what I can see happening now in your world, so that you will join with me and be hopeful. I have a different viewpoint from you, and can see many strands of hopeful energy and events that are separate at the moment, but will soon come together. They will join together as streams to form a mighty river; and create a river so mighty it will wash the world clean.

Where shall I begin to show you what I can see, and what I can feel as the beginnings of hope? I will begin with today and the years leading up to 2012.

2

Y OU MAY HAVE noticed the change in energy here lately, a combination of events has led some of you to despair, not hope. These events have been mostly to do with your economies and your personal financial arrangements and jobs. You fear for your future well-being as the economic collapse touches everyone on the planet. It was meant to touch everyone on the planet, to be a global correction of something gone badly wrong. It is catalysing change in your multi-national firms and banks that were so powerful they could do anything they wanted. There was little you as an individual could do against such power. Many of the things they do would appal you, and are very secret. Their business plans have been turned inward for so long; they have been only been focused on what will bring them more money and power. As their excesses have come to light, and their secrets have been laid bare all of the large corporations are weakened.

You have lived in countries that have been run for the benefit of these large businesses, who have told the governments how they must be treated or they will take their jobs elsewhere. They have been allowed free rein to despoil the land, and write the legislation under which they operate their businesses. The power structure is so entwined with these corporations that your elected representatives found they had little choice but to go along with them.

What have been the results from this governance? Look around at the state of the planet and the state of your health. You work hard and spend your money on food and drink that slowly kills you, and saps you of energy to make any changes. It takes a very strong person to go against the flow of your society, to live differently. Your homes are filled with useless objects that break and are discarded, and new ones are bought. You feel that if you stop buying your world will collapse. The manufacturers are busy making things that no one should waste time or resources making. They use up your planet's raw materials and energy to produce a great deal of junk.

Your economic shake-out is going to change this bleak picture that you have been living with for more than fifty years.

The new economies and corporations that arise will never be so large again. Their size has made them vulnerable to this crash, the future will belong to small to medium sized firms that are making the products that people need and want. There will be more contentment in the consumers of these items, and they won't have the low self-esteem that comes with wasting their money on rubbish. The party isn't over forever, but the party-goers will be drinking less.

I see hope here, as everyone returns to their senses. You have equated ownership of goods with happiness, without ever having a chance to find out what really makes people happy. Happiness is involvement with your own life, your families and friends. Buying things can't replace coming alive and living, using all those parts of you that you were born with. Happy are those who know what they are capable of and are out there living for their own satisfaction. When you create something good for yourself you are using that small part of you that is the Creator; you are finally being you.

You will find that your tolerance for being lied to and cheated by those who are manipulating you is gone. You mutter about this among yourselves, but you will begin to act and change your buying habits. "I'm not giving *them* my money." You will want a different world for yourself, and you will personally make your own changes to bring it about. The days before 2012 will be filled with people changing their spending habits, and without enough income those large corporations will close.

There is no inherent harm in making things and selling them to others, unless you are destroying the planet in the process. If you take one decorated shiny pink pottery pig for example, made from clay dug out of the ground in China, and the necessary fossil fuels used to make the electricity to fire it and for transport, that pig is not harmless. The world would be a better place without that pig sitting on someone's shelf, and later buried in a landfill. The people in China would have cleaner air and water without that pig, and ultimately healthier lives. Their main concern here is to have enough money to buy food and housing. The production of junk for overseas markets is not sustainable in any way ecologically or economically. Sometimes the creation of jobs for the sake of it has a bad effect. I would rather see these hard working people turn their hands and creativity to something they can take pride in and which will feed their families at the same time, and by this I mean some farming, fishing, small scale manufacturing, or theatre away from the big cities. We have come back to the balance of life in the largest cities, where it is difficult to feed families and judge when you have enough. It is always wanting more that is the problem, from the CEO of a large American corporation to the poor around the world.

What's wrong with always wanting more, why isn't that acceptable? Because your world population is so vast and overcrowded there isn't enough left for some of you to use so much and leave so little for others. Would you let a family member die for lack of food and water? Don't let your other selves die out of sight for the same reasons.

My reasons for hope are these: the groundswell of change has already started in the richest countries. I see enough light beginning to shine which is the light of truth, spotlighting those large corporations that have ruled you without your knowledge. These corporations will not be able to exist and sell their products when their workings have been laid bare. Really, it's that bad.

You will find more and more of these exposures during the economic downturn, the businesses are intertwined and as some of them fail they will take others with them. The remainder will have new legislation to end the manipulation of their accounting systems and be forced to stay in business under rules that are fair to all. This is important because these large corporations must be changed in their current forms so that the harm they do is ended. There will be an upturn in hope as people are empowered by the truth and there will be a new economy based on honesty and fairness. You used to have economies like that. Some of your citizens have been trying to inform you for years about what was happening, some have died but others were too well known, such as Ralph Nader. Now they will be supported in their efforts to shine a light into dubious practices. You will join to support people like this and you will trust them to help bring down these unfriendly corporations.

The next two or three years will bring about many changes so that the 2012 energy will strike a planet that is already in the process of renewal. You will be the ones who are making the adjustments and changes every day in your lives. When you act there is energy attached, when you act differently you have changed the energy, a stream has begun to flow to swell the river of change.

Energetically I am looking at malignant, stagnant corporations being undercut by a river of change. Think of buildings built on sand as the water washes away their foundations. When they are gone you will see that there is a lot left of a healthier, kinder, more honest type of business. These are the ones that have staying power.

I am the Archangel of Hope and I just spent pages talking about large corporations that I despise. You need to shift these out of your way before you can bring the light back into your national economies. And you will do exactly that. The downturn is a scouring and cleansing to rid you of these, and is a blessing of the hard kind. The majority of this restructuring will be completed by the year 2012. The thing about light is that it needs to bloom and blossom on this planet, and light can be anywhere and in anything. The same goes for the dark, and your corporations are bastions of darkness.

3

THESE DAYS BEFORE 2012 you have much to feel hope about. You are going to change the largest stumbling block there is in your world governance when the global corporations start to fall. When the countries start being run to suit the people living in them you will see a difference in each individual life. There will actually be more money to go around, and it is going to feel so different. Hope is twinned with Joy, if you remember her. She has had difficulty making her presence felt for these last decades. But she's back; she travels with me and as hope increases, joy increases. Joy, happiness, love, hope; will you really miss owning so many useless things if you have these? These are the real gifts of the universe.

These are days of darkness when you feel you don't know how you're going to keep food on the table, or how you're ever going to clean up the planet. These days last only until 2012, and steady change takes place every day that passes. By early 2012 you will be waking up in the mornings with a sense of anticipation over what new and good thing is going to happen that day. The hard work sorting out everything will be almost over, and progress will be underway on the world economies. They will have been put on new, firm foundations. Workers will be employed again on some of the same jobs, and some new and different ones. Hope that everything is picking up now will be widespread. Some of you will be feeling pretty happy as your excitement builds. I recommend that you trust me on this, and pin your hopes on the future.

I want you to feel as individuals that something wonderful is happening over the next few years. I want you to remember the good feeling that comes from spring cleaning your homes or emptying an overcrowded garage. This is the process you are going through now with your economies and you are all sharing the work, and one day you can all stand and admire the new society you have built together based on fairness. It will be a society where you can all participate together, where everyone has a feeling of belonging.

At this time in your various countries you are carrying large numbers of people who feel they are outside of the mainstream, that they are surplus to requirements and have no life-affirming roles. Many will deny this. The hopelessness of these people is part of what you are living with. You live together and you have this as part of your environment. Just as you have sun and rain, you have the energy of the people and animals that are part of your world forming the environment you live in. These vast numbers of people without hope have been formed by your societies, and now they are contributing hopelessness into the energetic mix. Are you your brother's keeper? If it is not your brother but part of yourself looking back at you through their eyes, then the answer must be yes.

These hopeless neighbours need to be acknowledged as your selves, your brothers and sisters. The changes that are taking place are for everyone to share in, and owning these strangers as yourselves, will help even out the highs and lows of wealth distribution. Give them your money? Not necessarily, but don't stand in their way of making what they can of their lives. Things will be changing faster than you can imagine. Who you see now as unemployable will not always be so. Just as the richest need to come closer to the middle, so do the poorest. Start in your own countries, and later look to even out wealth globally. The impetus and energy will be looking to do that, so you will be going with the flow. Some of these changes will be starting now, and picking up speed after 2012.

4

A T THIS TIME, pre-2012 one of the other changes that you will notice will be a rejection of poor food supplies. By this I mean that you will not choose to buy chemically tainted foods. These foods will become harder to sell as people begin to really see the lies behind the corporate selling strategies. Look to see the exponential growth of organic and local food. There will be less transport of food around the world, although the exotic foods will always be taken to the cold countries. What I'm talking about here is the normal fruits and vegetables, and goods like bottles of wine that circle the globe. These food air miles will decrease gradually as consumers realise they do not want to contribute to damaging themselves and the planet this way. Many will grow enough to contribute to what their households eat, even if in a small way. This will be important in the end, all those window boxes of lettuce and tomatoes. You can experience pleasure in picking something you grew yourself. We want you to find happiness in your lives, and small pleasures add up.

This all sounds so haphazard; I am asking you to take my word for a series of changes that are going to ignite your world in hope, by telling you to grow vegetables and fruit. You make the changes in your lives, and the changes multiply. What I see is the speed of the changes, and the rate of multiplication. It is all going to happen so fast, by the year 2012 some of you will have moved on to make changes that you will never reverse. Others will be slower, but like what they see in your lives and make their own changes at their own rate. By 2025 you will look back at the first ten years of the century and see how much has changed, and be happy that you were able to be part of it. Only a tiny few would go back if given the chance.

It's the beginning that is always hard, to change from one thing to something else. Once the changes have been made and a new way of living is established it runs along smoothly. You will have a time of two different ways of living co-existing side by side, but that will end. The other way just isn't sustainable. The new ways of living will be adopted by all in the end. I don't want to say any more about how you will be living, as sometimes one can say too much and limit what will take place. I wouldn't dream of limiting you. We all watch with excitement and great trust to see how you will correct the imbalances in your ways of living.

5

THE BIG YEAR ITSELF, 2012, will enter in with enough energy to push you all along with your changes. Think of yourselves dancing in the waves at a beach, and a large wave comes in and picks you up and sets you down closer to the shore. Just like that, you will all have moved using the power of the energy waves coming to Earth. But some of you will have been carried farther by the waves and found you were more ready for the jump. Then because it is so delightful you will be sure to be ready for the next wave and jump again. This is going to be a tremendous year for enlightened change, change with purpose and direction, inspired and assisted by light.

We have not forgotten that you are blindfolded and have trouble seeing which way to go, so we are going to be standing in the waves, our waves, and give you helping hands so you jump cleanly and don't go under. Some of us have been incarnating here for years and will use our own individual light as beacons to help guide you along. For those who wish to follow a path away from unhappiness there will be a clearly lit road. Your main task will be to understand what it is that makes you happy so you know which way to go. Remember we only deal in spiritual gifts, money is your problem and we have little to do with it.

The year will progress with minor miracles as more and more of you understand how to create something in your lives deliberately. There will be happy phone calls saying "I got that job I wanted so badly!", or "the retreat I planned has every place filled." This may start slowly, but you will remember how to do this as the year goes by. We are looking forward to these exciting days. More than these individual successes will be the people who are grouped together with one desire and purpose, and there will be progress finally on the cleaning of the Earth; and the end of her being despoiled. The core and beginning of the care of the Earth will be the healing groups you set up along the lines of those described as taking place in Atlantis. There's no reason to wait to set up yours.

6

2012 WILL ALSO be a time when people discover their power to force transparency in their governments. This is important because there are many things done in your name with your money that you will be very upset about when they come to light. Governments will find themselves under close scrutiny by the citizens. Not all elected officials are bad, but you have entrenched ways of doing government business that are inappropriate. By this I mean that harmful decisions are taken because they suit a small group of people, often large businesses and the very rich. Reclaiming your own right to fair government will be a sign of the change in energy. Many elected officials will help you with this, and others will run for cover. You have attracted people into power who are only there to get what they can for themselves or their friends. All steps to make it clear what is happening inside your governments are steps in the right direction.

Around that time when a large corporation applies for permission to dig up or despoil part of the Earth for their own profit, there will finally be a big "no". Where before you occasionally had a successful protest against destructive developments, there will be such a change in everyone's views that they will not be allowed to do so again. That is the day you are all waiting for, the day when you know the damage will not continue, and if you clean up there will not be more mess being created somewhere else. I can hear the sighs of relief now, and the new impetus to action will start from then.

That year will also bring about a boycott of some of the foods and drugs that are the least natural to put into your bodies. Some people will become so much healthier and vibrant by eating well so that they do not need to take pharmaceutical drugs to maintain health. They will cease to be customers of the global pharmaceutical companies as they are not ill. Now do you see how industries are intertwined? How poor food increases the profits of drug companies, because you cannot stay healthy on poor food sources. Let these drug companies help those who are seriously in need, not people who can't take the trouble to stay healthy with diet and exercise. The size of this particular industry worldwide is enormous. You would benefit if they were smaller and less powerful, as they're large enough to influence their own regulation.

What would it be like to have vibrant health? You would start by waking up with a spring in your step, with cheerful anticipation of what's happening that new day. When you feel good the small troubles and stresses have less effect on you. You are able to handle your day with ease and pleasure without feeling tired or lacking concentration. When you return home in the evening you enjoy preparing fresh food that helps you maintain this feeling, and have the energy in the evenings to do something recreational that you like, summer or winter. Because you have time for some fun relaxation you do not feel that your life is a treadmill of unpleasant work, and there is more balance. The current way of being so tired that you can't cook and just collapse after the evening meal is a sign of poor bodily health, leading to creative and mental imbalance. Finding balance, finding happiness and being active will be a new lease on life for so many of you. Life is to be enjoyed; it is the goal of all life. I want you to have hope, to see that even if you are not really enjoying your adult lives now that it is possible through diet, exercise and balance to change all of that. Remember Esmariel and ask for her help.

2012 will also create some crises where those things (of all sorts and descriptions) that are of the old energy will be pushed to the wall. Those new energy waves will come crashing in and some things that cannot change will stumble and fall, and go under. There will be some upheaval here, there and everywhere. Your own attitudes on change and how much you have used the run-up years to change your own lives will protect you from the worst of this. If you can handle the energy, and those of you who have gone back to healing yourselves daily will be in a good position, you will not be shaken up, but energised. You'll take that energy and use it for yourselves, families and the planet. It's like taking a fish out of water and finding that it's already adapted to dry land. These are going to be extraordinary days.

As the year proceeds month by month some of you will be leaping forward into life, you haven't had so much to experience and marvel at in years. There will be groups of you who are watching and celebrating the changes that are taking place. Where others go in fear of everything new and are trying to hold onto the past unsuccessfully, you will be skipping forward. There will appear to be two strands now, those embracing change and heading upwards, and those resisting change struggling on below. The energy of this year will do that.

This will be the year that is the beginning of the end for the population shifts into the large mega-cities globally. Those who are able to leave and move back into the country and smaller towns will begin a reverse migration. They will choose to move because they found that they would rather live where they can be closer to the Earth, to live where the energy is healthy and they feel good. This will further increase their health and well-being, and happiness. Remember that the Earth supports your feet and she will be stronger and more able to do this as each year goes by. Her absorption of the 2012 energy will make her effect on you stronger. Those who are able to move into contact with her will choose to relocate. The ever increasing pressure on the largest cities will start to ease and allow them to begin to cope with their populations for housing, clean water and transportation.

As the energy continues to build during the year the Earth itself will start to shake off the darkness lingering on her surface. This dark energy has been the mainstay and support for a lot of things that have happened here that have harmed you as human beings. So many of the things that have been mentioned that need to change have grown strong on this energy. The dark angels are going to resist it leaving the planet and look to find ways to keep it anchored. They will find it too hard to reattach it to the planet while she is shaking them off, so they may look to you as anchors. Beware of this, and keep your sights fixed on what is light and joy, and keep your own space and areas bright. When the year is over you will see more clearly where the darkness has anchored, and where you want to shine your many lights. This is the time to resist following along with others, but to measure everything against whether it brings joy, or hurts your fellow man.

I see a world washed clean at the end of the year, energetically clean finally as it has not been since those early Atlantean days. At the time of the destruction of Atlantis some of the darkness had travelled to the other continents, but nothing was ever so bad again as it was in Atlantis. When your world is cleaned and breathing through her skin, with the light of the sun touching her she will sparkle and grow in strength. That is the beginning of the days that will follow. Your role is to help her by anchoring the light yourself with your own bodies and energy fields and steady her all year long. This is what she needs from you to keep your contract with her.

7

THERE WILL BE some other changes resulting from the events of 2012. One will be that the governments, instead of slowing down the cleaning of the Earth will completely change direction and lead the way. It will be as if everyone who walks past a local toxic eyesore will suddenly demand to help clean it up and remove it. Not all of these will be toxic, but all will be offensive in some way. If it degrades the Earth it will have to be cleaned and repaired. (Did you see the movie WALL-E?) This work will begin in the wealthier western countries where the population is better informed. But even in the beginning money will be allocated to help the poorer countries begin their own cleaning and repair. The west will acknowledge their role in using these countries as dumps and start with those sites. Afterwards they will continue to help. This field of environmental cleaning will become a large industry for a number of years after 2012.

While the planet is being cleaned you will be going through a process of learning how to live differently. These days will have a little of the London Blitz magic about them as you all pull together with a common goal. They will be happy days with shared information and labour.

The other big energetic happening of the coming years is the removal of the veil so you can see the first five dimensions. This will allow you to be taught and helped by the planetary experts, the elemental kingdom of gnomes, fairies, dragons, etc. At first only some of you will see and speak with them, but I urge you to persevere and ignore the blind ones among you. You will need the elementals' help in the final stages of chemical and nuclear clean-up. They've been making a study of this over the years and they are ready to help you solve these tricky problems. You will work together. The future's going to be a little different than the present you are living in now.

These elementals are here to help the planet, and if they can help the planet by working with you that is exactly what they will do. No one need ever fear them. They are also able to look after themselves and I would warn you to be fair with them and treat them with respect. They are not to be mistreated in any way. This would seem an unnecessary thing to add, except we've watched how you treat animals and people you consider different from yourselves. Also your resident churches are going to have trouble fitting them into their descriptions of the rules to find God, and there is a potential for trouble from these organisations. And I see you, the vast majority of you, standing and protecting what you know to be right and true. The elementals will be happy to have you as partners in serving the Earth in this way.

Another change that follows 2012 will be the way you begin to treat your animals. There will be a gradual shift away from cruel farming and animal husbandry practices. People will want to know that they are eating an animal that has been well treated during its lifetime. This will actually be at the top of their list of priorities, instead of price, and there will be support from the government in the form of inspectors to help this along. Your governments are going to be so sane and reasonable, and responsive to the needs of the people, that you will be amazed.

Some of you have had good cause to worry about the children and young people over the past decades. There seems to be something wrong with them, with their increased unhappiness and inability to use their brains easily, unless they have been drugged by a doctor. They have lives where they don't learn how to interact with others, and they aren't socialised in the same way anymore. It can't all be done in school; some of it needs to be done in the playground. They need to spend more time with adults and other children and not alone with TV's or computer games, speaking through typed messages. This will all change. How? By changing the energy around them and pulling them away from the negativity that supports the above behaviour. You blame yourselves, your parents, your neighbours, everyone except the overall dark energy that supports the behaviour that harms your young.

If we could get you to really understand this, that everything is supported by energy, and when supported it thrives, and when there is no energy to support, it fails. This is a case of watching the energy flows, where are they going? If you can't see the energy flowing, you can see the results. When it seems like there is nothing one can do to resuscitate a failing business or organisation, then there is no energy going its way any longer. The quicker you are to realise this, the easier it is to know when to quit and turn your attention elsewhere. This is how your children's poor health and development skills have been supported by the darkness of the energy on this planet. That energy is going to change big time in 2012. There will be a return to joy for children, they will continue that joy of the very young their whole life long.

Finally, the biggest change of all for 2012 will be the increase in happiness and joy. You have lived without it for so long, on such meagre rations of joy that few of you even know what I'm talking about. Joy that resides in your hearts and bodies, that comes bubbling out in laughter and shared lives and loves is going to weave its way through your lives so that it is ever present. Joy will be found in your connection to others as you work side by side, joy in ending lives spent overworked in isolation and competition. The loneliness of the human soul has kept you always looking for more in so many ways. Did you ever wonder why you wish to accumulate so many possessions? The hole you are trying to fill is caused by your separation. The days that are coming will begin to knit you back together, some more quickly than others.

Joy and Hope are twins, and they travel with love, music, song and dance, laughter and truth. These are the new vibrations that are coming to your planet in 2012, as the universe will give of its best to its beloved planet. This planet will hold these, and embody them while you live on its surface. She will help you to become them too.

I hope that when you read all these changes that are coming that you understood that it will be harder to not change, than it will be for all of this to become part of your new world and lives. All that I have said will happen will be easy, just going with the flow of energy. Resisting, and trying to keep your societies exactly as they are will be so much harder than moving on into the future that is there for you. It will be one way for you to see who is anchoring dark or light, by watching how they squirm and try to hang on to everything as it disappears. In the end, over time, everyone will change; they won't be able to help it.

Remember that 2012 is the beginning year of a new world, a new planet Earth who is on the road to recovery and strength. She will recover thanks in some part to you, the universal energy waves, and others who love her including angels and elementals. This is going to be an era of teamwork, where the contributions of others and the rights of others to live their own lives even if they are of the plant and animal kingdom will be recognised. This will be a growing trend, every year adjustments will be made in how you think as a species. At some point down the line you will join with all of these other species and beings and you will become one in your consciousness, then you will all go together with the Earth when you ascend. Instead of single voices singing you will become a choir and sing together. I can hear the music now, and it is music of pure joy.

8

I AM THE ARCHANGEL of Hope, and part of my role is to find and create hope and fan the flames, and provide some oxygen so it can feed and grow. The previous section is meant to be taken seriously, as a view of a better world and life for you all; different from this current life with its overriding emphasis on what will make you individually happy. This is the future that I see for you when the corrections of the present time have been completed. The corrections will be progressing throughout the year of 2012, and it is best not to count on them restoring everything to a point in the past, say 2008. That is not a correction. Your societies will be changing so dramatically, with so much more warmth and love for every person. This will be a correction indeed, where everyone is cared for with love from the old to the young, the rich and poor, healthy and sick. You used to live like this.

When the year of 2012 has ended you will have some years of changeableness, with variations of progress from place to place and year to year. You will make progress, but the progress may not be steady. The years will go by with adjustments being made by everyone; ten years, twenty years, a few more. By then there will be such differences in how you are all living it will be as if five hundred years had gone by. Remember how people were living five hundred years ago? Imagine the kind of change that is waiting for you in the next decades. Embrace the changes and go with them. It's going to be a fascinating time to be alive.

There are many reading this that are feeling uneasy about so much change. You all have a tendency to resist change and hang onto the past, whether it is good or bad. When you are afraid that the future facing you could be worse than the present you have, you want to hang on to the present. That's why we are writing this book, to inform you so that you won't be so afraid of the coming changes. We don't want you to be afraid of the new future; we hope you will be excited about it. It's coming anyway, and if you want to move into it easily it will be by making the little changes in your lives as they come along. Even those so rigid that they cannot do this easily, will still make the changes and have the future.

They won't be able to block it from their lives. Your ability to change will make it easier for you, and your changes will affect everyone else. Stepping into the unknown can be exhilarating, remember what that feels like? It's a good feeling.

9

THIS BOOK HAS been about energy, the primeval force in the universe. First came the energy for creation, then the creation itself. On your world it is the same, first comes the energy to heal, to change, to hope, then the concrete results. Nothing happens without being initiated by energy.

Your ideas and hopes are sent into the higher dimensions where they collect and drop like rain into the middle and lower dimensions. By the time they coalesce into your lives the energy will make something real for you. This is why it is important to cancel negative thoughts such as "I'll never get a job", or "good things happen to everyone except me." You send these negative messages into the higher dimensions and they come back and create your life. "I cancel that negative thought" is one of the most effective things you can get used to doing in your lives. The second is to make happy, joyful thoughts and let them fall into your reality. "Good things always happen to me, everything always seems to work out ok." "I always meet such nice people." This is how the universe works, and this is how you are creating your lives.

We've been talking about you as part of your Creator with the power to make the life you want. We wanted to give you those examples so that you could get started on making lives that are happy. This is the beginning of using your power for yourself. One day we know many of you will move on past this first stage as the inspiration for further creating comes to you. Esmariel spoke of turning energy into matter, and matter into energy, and this is how you can do it for yourself. She will help you expand on the above ways of creating, and learn more about how to transform yourself. When more of you are busy powerfully creating happy lives for yourselves you will change the lives around you faster and faster. This is something that you can all do to help over the next years. It will make everything move more quickly and easily. And some of you are already very powerful creators now, creating unhappiness by brooding on negative things in your lives, and others have found they've got the hang of making their lives happy and 'lucky'. Good things can happen to everyone if you understand how it's done.

This is what we all want for you, to have good things happen in your lives, and for you to be happy. That's the kind of energy that we resonate with, and we carry the energy of love and joy because they are the same thing. In the last century on your planet we have seen too little joy, and so much killing that we wondered how you had the will to get up in the mornings and keep going. By now you have no living memory of any other time or way of living. This is what we see coming back to you over the next few decades, a reversal of the despair you have all gotten so used to and that is found all around the globe.

Your own personal reversal of sadness and despair starts with your own thoughts, although it may seem too simple to be effective it is the only thing that will really work. You will have to get used to thinking in a new way to make a different life. We are back to change again, change towards happiness.

There is enough happiness to go around, there's enough for everyone. When you untie happiness from money there is an unlimited supply. The other thing about happiness is that it expands so quickly, and spreads so easily. You can catch it from each other, and share it with each other. You can snuggle down under it like a warm quilt and enjoy it in private, or join in with others. It's the oil that makes everything run smoothly, and eliminates petty arguments and violence. There's plenty of it out there right now, but it's not circulating very well. I see it circulating more and more freely, and building in quantity until love and joy fill everyone's lives. Everyone's.

When you think of being really, really happy now you see a beginning and an end, as if you could not spend so much time happy and need to confine it to a time and place. "The happiest day of my life" is one of those phrases that could read "Every day is so happy and contented and it's my pleasure to share this one with you." We want you to think of how happy some things make you, and imagine your whole life making you that happy all the time. If there is anyone out there that feels this is a little too much happiness, and you'd rather not feel happy like that, then I'm sorry because your life is going to be so good that you'll end up happy anyway. You will all go together, and you will all end up being happy, because love and joy cannot be divided. Only through love will you join together again as the one human soul.

The final reunion is still in the future, but the steps will go towards the point that you will all be aiming at now. If you want to speed up the process, make your own life joyful and share your love and joy with everyone. This is the natural result of knowing who you are and what your purpose is in being alive on this beautiful planet.

10

I HAVE BEEN GIVEN the final position in this book to speak because I am the harbinger of hope, I can see your beautiful future and I wish you to go towards it fearlessly. None of us wish to see you suffer any longer, because this human soul has torn itself apart and suffered so much in the past. You have travelled a long, long road since your hopeful beginnings when you were drawing up a contract with the Earth; and we can see the end of that road. The road will end in light for you and for this planet, and the about-face that you perform will begin in the year 2012. It took a long time for you to arrive here and live your many lives, and learn so many lessons, and the learning is going to be easier as more and more of you are able to share in clusters of mini-consciousnesses. These consciousnesses are only a faint glimmer now, but they will become more firm and established as the decades go by.

Respect for animals and plants will also help you to move on, as they are your partners here, not your servants. The most obvious plants that will strike a chord with you are trees; you may be able to understand plants better if you look at how you treat trees and their ecosystems. 'Tree-huggers' is used as a term of derision here, but they are more in tune with the angelic orders than those who have no respect for other living beings.

The motivation for writing this book was the nearness of 2012; our love for you and the Earth, and for the other beings living here. You are not aware of the work done by the other species as they work as one to help the Earth; you think they are not capable of anything. This is very far from true. They have done much over the years to help her stay healthy and alive, and there are no animals or insects hoodwinked by the dark angels. These all deserve your respect and co-operation and a space to live. You do not care to share your lives too closely with insects, but they are particular favourites of ours. They are cheerful and lively and true to the light always. We would like to see you try to put them out-of-doors when you catch them inside your houses as much as you are able to out of respect. This is not always possible I know, but sometimes it is.

Did you know that you could try to set boundaries with them? It can help if you specify your home as yours, and ask them to leave and live outside. It can work better for some than others; it depends on how you put your energy and authority into it.

There was a time when you learned much from the insect elementals, and they are considering their return now to help again. It's been a long time since they were here on this planet.

You are very close now to the death of your great oceans. They are underwater deserts worse than the ones you have created on dry land, for they are so much larger. The myriad forms of life that once lived there have shrunk to a tiny percentage of the original, and this is all from the changes you have brought to the ocean by over-fishing, the way you fish, and the new acidity of the water itself. There aren't many years left to it. Of all your environmental crises, this is the one that will hurt you the most and it is the one that may be hardest to correct. Those who work to keep the oceans alive are those wonderful beings the swimming mammals; the whale and the dolphin families. They are more than dumb animals, they are beings of light. If you knew how much they are doing to try to continually balance the oceans you would never harm another one. If there is any saving of the oceans it will be because of their presence there singing and balancing, and monitoring the flows of energy. Just because you chose to be veiled doesn't mean anyone else did.

These great bodies of water are the reason you are blessed with a gentle land to live on, as they provide the water for your rain. The health of the oceans relies on the lives being lived in it to a far greater degree than the land does. There is a stirring around of water and energy by all the swimming through the depths of the different fishes and other creatures. It is maintaining the flow, as opposed to letting it go stagnant. Look at some of your large dead inland lakes that have been polluted to the point of dying. They are virtually lifeless, and have no life energy to share with you or the surrounding countryside. It all matters, the life and energy of everything matters to the whole. If you allow your oceans to approach the lifelessness of these dead lakes you will not have the energetic means of survival.

In the past you have reclaimed some dying lakes and rivers in North America. This is an important example to remember and share with other countries that have their own dying lakes and rivers. It is a focal point for all of you to start with, your treatment of water on your planet. I wanted to point this out now, so that when you are cleaning and preventing further pollution, a good number of you can be cleaning the water. In fact, I would recommend starting with air and water pollution for clean-up. I would also fight for tighter controls on polluting industries; this is one of those hidden areas of government that you are not going to like when it comes to light.

Take some time now, in the years before 2012 to heal yourselves, heal the planet, and start fighting for an end to ruthless pollution that no one benefits from, except the polluter. And remember the reason for this is to let the Earth know that you are aware of her needs and you are willing to work to heal her, as much as to stop more damage. It will make it easier when everything accelerates if you have taken these beginning steps now.

My hope is that when some of you have finished with this book you will go out and form your circles for healing with those who already have been initiated into Reiki or use another healing form. These groups will be the ones interested enough to take that energy and use it for practical clean-up. That could be in the form of protesting, fund-raising, letter-writing or getting your hands dirty. Make a start and the 2012 energy will come and lift you higher. I'm counting on you.

This is the beginning of a new phase for the Earth. You've had a long time of wandering around with your blindfolds on, and that is going to change shortly. Your goal of finding God; and finding yourself as a living part of God is on track to happen as you originally hoped when you contracted for this game. It is not a guaranteed conclusion, and you can't give up and say the universe or the angels will fix it for us. We can't do that. We can return in books like these and try to teach you as we did in Atlantis. I have chosen to reveal to you that these dark days will not last forever if you are prepared to help rather than block the energy that is coming in. We have given you help in the form of telling you the most powerful, yet simple ways of healing and helping yourselves. We are here to help you when you ask for our help.

I am Hophriel, the Archangel of Hope. I carry hope in my wings, and as I wave them hope travels through your lives and soul. This is not the end, but the beginning.

The Downfall of Atlantis

The second book by the Archangelic Collective focuses on the abuse of science during the Fourth Age of Atlantis. Who lived in Atlantis and what was that continent like? What began the slide to the most spectacular destruction ever seen on Earth? What happened to the survivors and the new civilisations they helped establish? Why was this forgotten; remembered only as the stories of heroes and deeds of legends?

This book follows in time the previous book by the collective, Planet Earth Today, but is written to stand alone and be understood by any reader who has not read the earlier book. The information is not duplicated, for there is so much to say about the history of humanity on this planet without writing it twice.

The first section gives the history of the first three ages of Atlantis and the beginning of the slow slide towards the end. It is followed in the second section by a detailed history of how the scientific advancements of cloning stifled the souls of those alive in the Fourth Age. The cruelty of the Age led to a society so detrimental to man and planet that in the end the angels intervened. Only those who had held themselves aloof from the main societies escaped in ships.

The Atlantean influence on the formation of the African, Egyptian, Celtic, North American, Central American and other cultures is described; and what these cultures offered the Atlanteans. How were the great stone circles like Stonehenge made, and what was their purpose on all levels, and through all dimensions? Why do all timelines converge on the battle of Glastonbury Tor where Arthur and Merlin fought the last battle against the Shadow of the East?

The final section covers the Time of Legends where the whole story of Arthur and his importance is related, the world of dragons, elves and fairies, and the Ring which surfaces in the operas by Wagner and books by Tolkien, and more. Why is it impossible to remember this time, and how did it come to be hidden? What is the effect on people today that they have lost this part of their history?

The Archangels have chosen this time to shed light on these subjects because they themselves are beings of light. They wish to help the light to grow on this planet through understanding how these events came about, and reconsider our current support for all science whether beneficial or not.

ISBN 978-0-9565009-1-5
Available from Amazon.com and Amazon.co.uk.
www.candacecaddick.com

Lightning Source UK Ltd.
Milton Keynes UK
17 May 2010

154314UK00001B/6/P